Meaning in Absurdity

What bizarre phenomena can tell us about the nature of reality

Meaning in Absurdity

What bizarre phenomena can tell us
about the nature of reality

Bernardo Kastrup

BOOKS

Winchester, UK
Washington, USA

First published by iff Books, 2011
iff Books is an imprint of John Hunt Publishing Ltd., No. 3 East Street, Alresford,
Hampshire SO24 9EE, UK
office1@jhpbooks.net
www.johnhuntpublishing.com
www.iff-books.com

For distributor details and how to order please visit the 'Ordering' section on our website.

Text copyright: Bernardo Kastrup 2010, 2017

ISBN: 978 1 84694 859 6
978 1 84694 860 2 (ebook)

A CIP catalogue record for this book is available from the British Library.

Design: Stuart Davies

UK: Printed and bound by CPI Group (UK) Ltd, Croydon, CR0 4YY
US: Printed and bound by Thomson Shore, 7300 West Joy Road, Dexter, MI 48130

We operate a distinctive and ethical publishing philosophy in
all areas of our business, from our global network of authors to
production and worldwide distribution.

Contents

Other books by Bernardo Kastrup

Rationalist Spirituality:
An exploration of the meaning of life and existence informed by logic and science

Dreamed up Reality:
Diving into mind to uncover the astonishing hidden tale of nature

Why Materialism Is Baloney:
How true skeptics know there is no death and fathom answers to life, the universe, and everything

Brief Peeks Beyond:
Critical essays on metaphysics, neuroscience, free will, skepticism and culture

More Than Allegory:
On religious myth, truth and belief

Coming March 2019
The Idea of the World:
A multi-disciplinary argument for the mental nature of reality

To the absurd within us all

from ingrained structures of thought I had grown so identified with I could hardly conceive of any other legitimate avenue of thinking. Yet, this is precisely what I now believe this book to embody: a previously unthinkable but legitimate articulation of an uncanny scenario about the nature of reality. If my own experience while researching it is representative, this book may confront some of your dearest notions about truth and reason, just as it confronted mine. Yet, it may do so in a way that you cannot dismiss lightly, because the evidence it compiles and the philosophy it leverages are solid in the traditional, academic sense.

The most exciting discoveries always entail the loss of previously held certainties. So here is my invitation to you: This is a short and sharp book, wasting no space on non-essentials or divagations. Making your way through it will not demand any major investment of time or effort. So give it an honest chance, and it may just help you open up entirely new dimensions for exploring that ultimate of all questions: What is going on?

Chapter 1

The calls of the absurd

First call: It is the mid-1980s, in a remote valley in northern Europe. A strange light is seen in the dark night sky. Its observer cannot make sense of what he sees: the light bounces around and performs impossibly tight turns at extremely high speeds. Inertia would prevent any object with significant mass from performing such maneuvers. Yet, the phenomenon is sustained. Even more puzzling, the movements of the light do not appear to serve any purpose: its zigzagging trajectory is absurd. Nonetheless, there is little doubt about the physical reality of the phenomenon: clear footage of its manifestation is captured. Over the years, the lights return to the same valley and are consistently observed by countless witnesses. A wealth of physical evidence is accumulated: pictures, film, radar data, and traces left on the ground directly under where the lights had appeared.

Second call: North America, also in the mid-1980s, in the suburbs of a large city. This time, more than just a strange light haunts the skies: hundreds of people independently witness, over a period of years, an enormous formation of lights seemingly attached to a large V-shaped craft. Witnesses include scientists, engineers, police officers, and city administration officials. The consistency of the observation reports evokes theories of secret military craft and even extraterrestrial visitation. Yet, a passing comment by a key witness seems to suggest something far more profound than such provincial explanations: 'From beginning to end, the nineteen to twenty minutes that I have viewed that craft was also a time of self-examination of myself and who I was.' Some witnesses report a feeling that the strange light formation was somehow attempting to communicate with them.

Third call: Not all strange objects in the sky appear harmless. In the 1950s, a man stands observing the late afternoon sky. The sun is clearly visible behind a veil of clouds, just above the horizon. Suddenly, the sun becomes uncannily pale and what appears to be a second sun becomes visible at about the same height above the horizon. When the first sun sets, the second sphere of light speeds towards the Earth, as if falling from the sky. The man stands in awe of the spectacle. As the sphere approaches the moment of impact, the man realizes it is a much smaller object than he had initially thought. He also notices what appears to be decorative, symbolic markings on its surface. When the 'sun' finally crashes onto the Earth, it does so at a considerable distance from the man. Other similar spheres then appear, falling towards the ground just as the first did. The man fears possible shrapnel and runs away. As he does so, he suddenly finds himself inside a house, where a girl sits in a chair with a large notebook on her lap. He tries to convince her to flee with him, but she will have none of it.

Fourth call: The theme of suns falling from the sky is a recurrent one. Early in the 20th century, in southern Europe, tens of thousands of people gather in a field. After a downpour, the storm clouds break and the sun becomes visible again. However, it has the uncanny aspect of a spinning disk, looking paler and duller than normal. Without notice, it careers towards the Earth in a kind of absurd, zigzag trajectory, frightening all present. Afterwards, witnesses observe that the muddy puddles of water on the ground, as well as their previously soaked clothes, had all suddenly become dry. The phenomenon, due to its simultaneous physical palpability and absurdity, confuses scientists and commentators for decades thereafter.

Fifth call: Not all calls of the absurd involve merely strange objects in the sky; some involve living entities. Moreover, some stories go beyond mere non-compliance to the known laws of physics; *they defy something much more fundamental: logic itself*. A man in North America recounts seeing several weird entities, which he describes as 'elves,' at the side of a road he travels regularly. One of them paralyzes him, while others hold up placards displaying beautiful, moving geometric forms, presumably as he whizzes by in his car. He feels that the 'elves' want him to look at these abstract images. The entire situation is clearly nonsensical: elves at the side of a road, forcing a driver to watch the unfolding of abstract geometric forms while paralyzed at the wheel of a car? What is the sense of that? Yet the man is unlikely to be lying, for his report was part of a carefully controlled study.

By now, you may be tempted to recoil from all this nonsense with a dismissive wave of the hand. But bear with me a little more: clearly, these are not *literally real* events. Still, I will be contending that they may, nonetheless, be exceedingly important to our understanding of what we call reality.

Sixth call: Springtime in North America, in the 1960s. A man steps out of his house and comes face to face with a saucer-shaped object hovering above his yard. A hatch opens and the man sees three entities inside the craft. The supposed aliens are small and dark-skinned, like certain types of fairies. One of the entities holds up a jug to the man, a gesture the man interprets as a request for some water. Space aliens, able to fly undetected across solar systems, needing to stop by and reveal themselves to a man in order to fill up a jug of water? What is the logic of that? Nonetheless, the man obliges, filling the jug with water from inside his house. When he returns, he sees one of the entities inside the craft frying what appears to be food on a kind of grill. Upon taking note of the man's interest in their food, one of the entities hands the man three pancakes. Thereafter, the entities close the hatch, take off, and disappear. Naturally, it would be easy to dismiss such story as the delusions of a pathological mind, especially given the fact that no physical evidence could be found upon further investigation; that is, except for the pancakes, which were sent by the United States Air Force for analysis at the Food and Drug Laboratory of the United States Department of Health, Education, and Welfare.

Seventh call: A man claims to be abducted by space aliens. These aliens seemingly take people, against their will, into their spaceships. The man is in one such a spaceship when the lights are suddenly dimmed. He looks up to his left and sees a very bright image of a jagged cliff. A magnificent bird is perched on top of this cliff, radiating an intensely bright light. The man is overwhelmed by this image and filled with awe. The aliens on the ship stop all their activities to watch the bird along with the man. All are transfixed. The bird opens its majestic wings and is suddenly gone. All activities in the ship then resume. It seems highly *illogical* that a *very terrestrial symbol*, such as a bird, could be so dear to aliens from outer space. Indeed, upon later reflection, the symbolic nature of the entire event was clear to the man, although he was apparently still able to somehow reconcile this realization with his belief in the literal reality of his experience.

I will close this brief anthology of the absurd with an account that I, personally, consider a unique gem; not so much for the caliber and stature of the man in question, but for the profound, mesmerizing metaphorical significance of his experience.

Eighth call: A man stands in a dark underground cave, whose entrance is guarded by a dwarf. He is afraid, but *intuitively feels* that he must penetrate deeper into the cave, until he arrives at a kind of inner chamber. There lies a strange, luminous red stone. The man takes the stone in his hands and realizes that it covers an opening in the underlying rock. Peering through the opening, the man sees water flowing at the bottom of another, yet deeper underground chamber. Submerged in the stream he sees a bright red light, which he describes as a sun, radiating through the water, with serpents swimming around it.

* * *

The stories above are very different from one another. Yet, I trust you will have noticed some common themes between them: their defiance not only of the known laws of physics but – and much more significantly – those of logic and common sense as well; their highly symbolic, metaphorical, psychological character; strong and unexplained intuitions seizing the subject at a deep emotional level; and the occurrence of common motifs such as fairy-like entities (aliens, dwarfs, elves), aerial phenomena, zigzagging motion, the sun, and other radiating light sources. These commonalities are indeed surprising when one considers the drastically different origins of these stories. I have deliberately veiled their specifics so you could consider them without prejudice at first. But it is now time to lift the veil.

Each of the eight 'calls of the absurd' above relates a different story. The story of the moving light in the first call comes from an observation of an unidentified aerial phenomenon made in 1986, in the Hessdalen valley of central Norway. Tantalizing footage was taken of that observation and later made available on the Internet.[1] In the years that followed, repeated observations of the same strange light-phenomenon have been made by a staggering number of witnesses in the very same valley. The consistency and repeatability of the phenomenon in a well-defined geographic location – a rare characteristic among unidentified aerial phenomena – eventually attracted the interest of scientists. Their involvement – and the instruments and methods they brought to bear – has now led to the accumulation of a wealth of physical evidence.

Indeed, the lights at Hessdalen are, from a scientific

standpoint, a veritable jackpot among all unidentified aerial phenomena *and*, incomprehensibly, one of the least known and written about. Because the phenomenon can be reliably expected to occur at a precise location, scientists have had the chance to mount several expeditions to the locale, bringing in and setting up myriad cameras, sensors, and other scientific instruments. Even an automatic monitoring station, equipped with a video camera, has been set up at the top of a hill overlooking the valley. The idea was to snap footage of the phenomenon even if it occurred while the scientists were not around. Sure enough, perhaps the best and clearest footage ever captured of an unidentified aerial phenomenon has been taken by this camera.

The justification for investing in the study of the Hessdalen phenomenon has been the possibility that it represents a new and yet unknown form of energy, which could potentially be harvested. Several scientific papers have been published on the lights. Much of the speculation centers on some form of plasma generated by atmospheric ionization of air and dust.[2] The cause of the ionization is not understood. An interesting study concluded that 'analysis of video frames and radar echoes showed that light spheres emerged "out of thin air" like a standing wave that ionizes the air in its maximum points.'[3] The origin of the standing wave is unclear. Though plasma theories seem to explain some aspects of the phenomenon, a survey concluded that 'several obscure aspects still remain and demand more in-depth investigation.'[4] To this day, no definitive explanation has been found for the Hessdalen lights, despite its continuing occurrence. A researcher concluded in resignation, after years of investigation, that 'this light phenomenon is *elusive* and its behavior most often *unpredictable*'[5] (emphasis added). The same researcher had earlier stated, in apparent frustration with the extraterrestrial visitation hypothesis often associated with the phenomenon, that 'whatever these things are, if some "alien intelligence" is behind the Hessdalen phenomenon, that hypothetical intelligence has shown no interest in searching a direct, continuative and structurally evolved communication with mankind and went on behaving in such a way that the light-phenomenon itself appears to be *totally elusive*'[6] (emphasis added). In the next chapter, we will consider the curious elusiveness that calls of the absurd seem to have built into them, as if elusiveness and self-negation were inherent in their manifestation. Whatever the case, the fact of the matter is 'that the [Hessdalen] phenomenon, whatever it is, can be measured.'[7] *So its elusiveness certainly does not mean that the phenomenon is not physical in nature.*

The second call of the absurd is actually the well-known 'Hudson valley UFO sightings,' a wave of sightings of unidentified aerial phenomena during the 1980s and '90s, along the Hudson river valley in New York state.[8] Thousands of witnesses described seeing similarly shaped flying craft or light formations. An investigation of these sightings was apparently the last UFO-related work of the late Dr. J. Allen Hynek, perhaps the best-known and most respected UFO researcher to date. My motivation for mentioning this story here is not so much the physical evidence the phenomenon may have left behind, but the fact that so many witnesses have independently made consistent observations of it. Something else that I find even more significant is *the introspective, psychological aspect of the phenomenon*. This last point is substantiated by a segment of an interview given to a television station by Dennis Sant, one of the key witnesses, whom I quoted earlier in this chapter. Indeed, it is intriguing and logically unexpected that the sight of what he supposed to be a craft would have triggered introspective self-reflection about his own identity. If I *literally* saw a strange craft I guess much would go through my mind, but not questions about my own nature.

The two cases above – namely, the Hessdalen lights and the Hudson valley sightings – underscore the apparent objectivity of the phenomena described. In the Hessdalen valley case a wealth of objective measurements have been taken, which include spectrographic analyses, radar echoes, photographs, laser data, and even analyses of soil samples. The Hudson valley case highlights the fact that multiple witnesses, of very different backgrounds and independently of one another, were able to describe quite similar sightings. This corroborates the hypothesis that, despite the fact that the phenomenon did have a clear psychological component, whatever it was that the witnesses were observing was not 'just in their heads.'

Sometimes, however, the observations are entirely subjective. Indeed, the story of the third call of the absurd is, in fact, a dream reported to psychiatrist Carl Jung around the middle of the 20th century.[9] Jung interpreted the 'suns' in the dream as symbols of a balanced, fully integrated psyche (which he called the 'Self'), a goal the dreamer had not yet achieved. Since this goal entails bringing into awareness aspects of the personality that many of us would rather not acknowledge or confront, the dreamer's 'unconscious' mind projected it onto the pictorial symbol of external suns. (Although I consider the word 'unconscious' inaccurate, since it refers to mental contents that may still entail phenomenal properties despite being inaccessible to metacognitive introspection, I shall continue to use it throughout this book, without scare quotes, for the sake of readability and consistency with depth psychology literature. This should be seen as an hesitant *concession* on my part, not as an acknowledgement of the appropriateness of the word.) The fact that the suns were crashing onto the ground represented, still according to Jung, the drive for the integration of this unconscious impulse into the world of ego-consciousness represented by the Earth. That such integration came accompanied by the potential danger of a cosmic bombardment was the natural reaction of the dreamer's ego-consciousness, apprehensive as it was of becoming aware of unwelcome aspects of the dreamer's personality. That said, the girl the dreamer meets while attempting to flee clearly does not acknowledge the potential risks: she chooses to stay behind and continue whatever work she was carrying out with her notebook. Jung interpreted the figure of the girl as the Anima, the unconscious female component of the dreamer's psyche, who knew there was in fact no danger. As it turns out, the Anima appears to have been correct, for the 'suns' crashed far enough away from the dreamer that no harm was ultimately done.

In Jung's book on flying saucers,[10] he elaborates extensively on the idea that 'lights in the sky' are a projection of an unconscious desire for wholeness; a desire that entails becoming aware of aspects of ourselves that we reject and, therefore, can only express by projecting this desire outside of ourselves. Jung, however, does not deny the physical evidence of some 'flying saucer' observations (for instance, radar echoes), offering two conceptual frameworks to account for it. First, he conjectures that a physical, external event may trigger a projection by the unconscious mind of the observer. In other words, the witness 'dresses' a real object in the sky with the symbolic fantasy of the unconscious. Second, Jung appeals to the concept of synchronicity, which he developed together with physicist Wolfgang Pauli.[11] The idea here is that an unconscious psychic impulse may occur together with a physical, real event consistent with the psychic impulse, even though there is no causal relationship between the two. In other words, synchronistic events are the results of a kind of acausal 'orderedness' in nature. Just as two events can be related to each other by a causal relationship, synchronicity postulates that they can also be related by a *meaning relationship* resulting from an underlying network of meaningful connections in nature. In this framework, the *physically real*, unidentified aerial phenomenon would be a synchronistic manifestation in the external world accompanying the unconscious process taking place in the witness's psyche. Naturally, the idea of synchronicity has no clear basis in modern physics, the latter being fundamentally grounded in causality.

The fourth call of the absurd is so similar to the dream discussed above that you would be excused for assuming it was also a dream. After all, the exact same theme of the sun turning pale and falling towards the Earth – this time in a zigzag trajectory, like the Hessdalen phenomenon – is found there too. So it may surprise you that, in fact, the story narrated there is a summary of the world-famous 1917 'Miracle of the Sun' at Fátima, Portugal.[12] A crowd of tens of thousands of people had assembled because of claims by three shepherd children that the Blessed Virgin Mary had appeared to them on multiple earlier occasions and had promised a miracle at that precise location and time. The narration of the fourth call comprises the highlights of the events that ensued. The sheer number and geographical distribution of the witnesses involved seem to render any interpretation purely along the lines of a delusion untenable. *Something objective happened at Fátima*, even if strong psychological aspects were integral to the story – as was clearly the case, in view of our earlier discussion of the dream experienced by Jung's patient.

The events outlined in the fifth call of the absurd kick it up a notch as far as sheer weirdness is concerned, for the story now includes living entities of a bizarre nature. It will thus likely come as a relief to you that these were visions induced in a human volunteer by a powerful psychoactive substance (N,N-dimethyltryptamine, or DMT), during a clinical study at the University of New Mexico's School of Medicine.[13] Indeed, the literature on the phenomenology of hallucinogenic substances is awash with references to entities often described as 'elves,' 'fairies,' and 'aliens,'[14] so this kind of report is fairly typical and representative of a much larger volume of data.

The volunteer in this case had the visions while lying safely in a hospital bed, under the supervision of medical staff. His experience was, therefore, entirely mental – he certainly was not driving his car on a road. Nonetheless, many of the volunteers of this clinical study insisted that the visions they had were not mere delusions or hallucinations, but were *real* – in fact, 'more real than real' was their characterization.[15] These were psychiatrically screened, sound-minded people who were perfectly aware that they were lying in a hospital and being injected with a psychoactive drug. And yet they could not shake off the 'overwhelming and convincing sense of certainty' they seem to have come back with regarding the reality of their experiences.[16] Clearly, that reality could not have been the same as our everyday physical reality. A Jungian interpretation of what might have happened is that the drug allowed the volunteers access to the contents of the personal and collective unconscious segments of their mind. I will discuss these concepts of Jungian psychology at length later on but, for now, the message I want to stress is this: *When the symbolic, metaphorical, often absurd contents of the unconscious parts of the psyche emerge into consciousness, they feel at least as real as the physical world around us.*

'Elves,' 'fairies,' and 'aliens' are most certainly not the exclusive domain of drug-assisted expeditions into the unconscious. The story narrated in the sixth call of the absurd is that of Joe Simonton, perhaps the last person one would expect to be under the influence of such psychoactive compounds. No, whatever Joe experienced, he experienced it without the help of hallucinogenic chemicals. And there is no denying how convincingly real it felt to him.

Joe Simonton's case was analyzed and reported by respected French UFO investigator Dr. Jacques Vallée in 1970.[17] As it turns out, the pancakes that the 'aliens' supposedly gave Joe were made of perfectly regular earthly ingredients. *Puzzlingly, however, they did not contain any salt.* As Vallée stresses, Joe Simonton was considered a very reliable, sincere, and trustworthy man, this being the reason why even the Air Force took his original claims so seriously. Vallée then goes on to compare Joe's experience with old fairy stories from Celtic folklore. As it turns out, there is a wealth of folk stories where the fairies either offer or ask for food. Interestingly, *fairies never eat salt*. Vallée makes an elaborate and convincing case for the relationship between modern encounters with 'aliens' and old fairy lore. He suggests persuasively that 'aliens' and 'spaceships' may be simply the modern ego's interpretation of the same underlying stimulus that inspired the original folk stories about fairies and elves.[18] More recently, journalist Graham Hancock articulated a similar case for linking fairy lore with the modern alien abduction phenomenon, as well as with psychedelic experiences.[19] The similarities are indeed difficult to dismiss as mere coincidences. If these authors are correct, then there is nothing really new or modern about UFO sightings, alien abductions, or the elves of psychedelic trances. These may all be modern reinterpretations of a mysterious phenomenon perhaps as old as humankind itself.

Since we find ourselves already on the subject of alien abductions, let us now look into the case described in the seventh call of the absurd. The man in question is Jim Sparks, a patient of the late Harvard psychiatrist Dr. John E. Mack. Dr. Mack reported on this case in his second and last book on the abduction phenomenon.[20] He wrote that his patients, despite acknowledging the apparently absurd elements in their stories, believed strongly in the *objective reality* of their abduction experiences. Such cognitive dissonance is reminiscent of the reports of the DMT study volunteers discussed above. Although Dr. Mack was known (and ridiculed) for taking his patients seriously, his book clearly suggests that, in his own view, the 'reality' of his patients' experiences was unlikely to be the same physical reality we ordinarily experience. Because Dr. Mack, as a trained physician, could find no clinical basis for dismissing his patients' claims as either delusions or lies, he found himself struggling to locate new ontological ground that could somehow account for their claims. He freely speculated about the possible existence of other dimensions of space-time, whose phenomenality may, under certain circumstances or particular states of consciousness, intersect our normal continuum.[21] He acknowledged the strong metaphorical, symbolic aspects of his patients' experiences. Indeed, any psychologist would be able to easily formulate a solid psychological interpretation of the symbolism of a glowing majestic bird, as recounted by Jim Sparks. Running out of options to make sense of these conflicting aspects of the clinical data in front of him, Dr. Mack further speculated about *a realm of reality that could violate the strict separation between the subjective, psychological world inside our mind, and the objective, physical world 'out there.'*[22] This would be the only way he could explain how patients who displayed no mental pathology and no signs of deception could swear by absurd, illogical stories loaded with undeniable psychological symbolism.

We now come to the eighth and last call of the absurd. What is recounted there were the experiences of Carl Jung himself, in a vision – not a dream – he had on December 12, 1913, presumably while sitting alone at night, in his study.[23] The record of this and many others of Jung's visions was finally published in 2009, almost 50 years after his death in 1961. It recounts a magical, rich, profoundly meaningful journey through Jung's personal unconscious, as well as through the collective unconscious. Jung's ability to dive so deep into his own mind was astounding, and most certainly a key element of his genius in understanding, explaining, and ultimately curing the human mind of its many ailments. His many expeditions into the unconscious reveal a world of symbol, metaphor, chaos, incongruity, paradox, and myth; a world populated by many *autonomous entities* whom Jung named and became acquainted with over the years. He would later explain that the basis for much of his psychological theories was born out of 'discussions' with these seemingly autonomous characters.[24] Among them was a *flying, winged man* he called 'Philemon,' who helped Jung realize that there is such a thing as *psychic objectivity*, or 'the reality of the psyche;'[25] that there were parts of the mind that had an autonomous existence and were not under his ego's control; parts that coalesced into a kind of internal reality, a populated universe that did not obey the laws of physics *or logic* to which the external world seems forever subject.

Jung extensively analyzed his own visions and fantasies. He interpreted his expedition into the cave, recounted earlier, as a metaphorical descent into the depths of the unconscious mind, where chaos and absurdity reign, but which are nonetheless bursting with meaning. There, surrounded by dark and threatening symbols, he found a new sun; a red sun of the depths that sheds new light on humanity and bestows wondrous insights inaccessible to the rational, logical ego-consciousness of the psychic surface.[26]

What can we make of all this? In a way, this is the exploration of this book. But we have just begun, and at this point it would be premature to attempt any conclusion. What we can do at this stage is to summarize a few observations from the discussion above: Calls of the absurd can be physical and measurable in nature – even if elusive – as we have seen when discussing the Hessdalen lights. They can also be objective in the sense that multiple and independent observers often report consistent descriptions of their manifestation, as in the case of the Hudson valley sightings. Calls of the absurd – even when objective – have a puzzling tendency to induce introspection and trigger intuitive insights, as the interview with Dennis Sant revealed. Sometimes this introspective nature is evident in the symbolism of a dream, as was the case with the experiences of Jung's patient. Surprisingly, these very symbolisms seem to sometimes 'spill out' into the objective world, as with the Miracle of the Sun at Fátima. Even seemingly autonomous entities can be part of these absurd scenarios, whether they are unambiguously mental manifestations (as was clearly the case for our DMT study volunteer) or are perceived as part of physical reality (as

Joe Simonton believed). Finally, Jung's own expeditions into the unconscious revealed to him the animated, autonomous nature of the depths of the human psyche, which can assume the form of absurd entities, paradoxical scenarios and storylines to convey a symbolic, poignant experience beyond logical apprehension.

Chapter 2

The elusiveness of the absurd

Investigators of calls of the absurd have systematically sought rational explanations for these phenomena. The underlying assumption was so self-evident it hardly needed to be made explicit: whatever the phenomena were, their causes had to be rooted in logic and physics. Thus the most elusive evidence and the most absurd testimonies – those that demonstrably required a violation of the established laws of physics to hold true, or which were nonsensical on the face of it – could be nothing but fabrications or delusions and were, therefore, dismissed.

It was not until the 1970s that Jacques Vallée realized that it was precisely the elusiveness of certain pieces of evidence and the absurdity of certain reports – the violation of physics and common sense they implied – that rendered them most interesting for study.[1] He understood that if these reports were not outright lies then their significance was considerable. Vallée is the true pioneer of the empirical study of the absurd as something beyond psychology; the first to open the door to a whole new way of thinking about strange observations of the world 'out there.' Our culture may, in the not-so-distant future, have much to thank Vallée for.

In his book *The Invisible College*, Vallée noted that many UFO observations entailed a kind of 'recursive unsolvability:' the phenomenon negated and contradicted itself, whatever explanation for it one came up with. Not only were the testimonies illogical and misleading, even the physical evidence left behind was ambiguous and elusive. He acknowledged that the lack of logic behind the phenomenon made one feel tempted to place it beyond rationality.[2] Yet, the inclination to dismiss the weirdest cases seemed unwarranted to Vallée. Referring to previous work done by Dr. J. Allen Hynek, Vallée noted that the strangeness of a report did not correlate with lack of reliability on the part of its witness. In fact, often the weirdest testimonies originated from the most reliable witnesses.[3] Something intriguing was going on. Vallée realized, from the study of the countless cases he had privileged access to, that the reality of the phenomenon appeared to be *both* physical and psychic *at the same time*.[4] In more recent work, he reaffirmed this conclusion and proceeded to lay out a phenomenological classification scheme encompassing six layers: a physical layer, an anti-physical layer (capturing the aspects of the phenomenon that contradict currently understood physics), a socio-psychological layer, a physiological layer (capturing observed alterations of the witnesses' bodily functions), a psychic layer (in the parapsychological sense), and a cultural layer.[5] In this same work, Vallée suggested that the phenomenon indicates the need for new models of physical reality. Indeed, Vallée is well known for taking the position that the so-called 'extraterrestrial visitation hypothesis' is insufficient to explain the scope of strangeness of the calls of the absurd.[6]

Perhaps the most controversial of Vallée's conclusions is that there is a *purpose* behind the occurrence of these strange phenomena. Having tried in vain to find a closed, sensible, logical explanation for UFOs for many years, Vallée concluded that the right question to ask was not where the UFOs came from, *but what effect they were causing*. This latter question could be answered empirically based on relatively straightforward research. His conclusion: *the calls of the absurd are leading to a shift in human consciousness and our conception of reality*. He empirically observed a seeming schedule of reinforcement that works to cement this shift over time.[7] Nonetheless, Vallée then left it open whether such a shift is caused by premeditated action by an intelligent agency, or whether it is simply the result of natural laws yet to be discovered.[8]

However, by the time he wrote *Messengers of Deception*,[9]

Vallée's position had become more influenced by conspiracy-related hypotheses. He took the ambiguity, self-negation, and contradiction always present in the calls of the absurd not as natural, inherent properties of the phenomenon, but as devices designed to influence human culture through confusion and misleading signals. Personally, I find this shift in Vallée's thinking unfortunate. To me, the explanation that requires the fewest assumptions is that ambiguity is an inherent and natural aspect of the calls of the absurd, not the result of a Machiavellian intervention in human culture.

Decades after Vallée began his investigations into UFOs and other related phenomena, Harvard's Dr. John Mack became interested in the so-called 'alien abduction' phenomenon. As a psychiatrist, his original interest likely had psychological motivations. However, having failed to uncover a purely medical explanation for the reports of his patients, Dr. Mack ventured carefully into the territory of speculative ontology. His observations are uncannily consistent with Vallée's own. He talks of the concurrently psychic and objective nature of the phenomenon, as well as of its elusiveness. He speaks of a 'third zone' that violates the boundaries between the subjective world of mind and the objective world of matter 'out there.'[10] He even suggests that the phenomenon is 'designed' – not necessarily in a teleological sense, but rather in a compensatory and spontaneous manner – to break down this separation between subjective and objective worlds and to force the experiencers to confront the inadequacy of the worldviews they have hitherto held.[11] He speaks of 'ontological shock'[12] as the mechanism by which the phenomenon forces an expansion of people's conception of reality towards a worldview where notions previously held to be absurd become intelligible. In interviews he conducted with shamans from pre-literary cultures of Africa and South America, Dr. Mack asked whether the alien- or fairy-like entities they claimed to have dealings with were supposed to be literal creatures or simply metaphors. He was then told that, according to the worldviews of these pre-literary cultures, there was no difference between the two;[13] certainly a very counterintuitive reply for the Western mind to assimilate. Nonetheless, by the end of this book, it will hopefully become clearer what those shamans might have meant when they spoke of an identity between the literal and the metaphorical.

It is remarkable how, based on an entirely different and more recent set of data, Dr. Mack arrived at very similar speculations to those originally put forward by Vallée. Indeed, yet another investigator of 'funny things' has also arrived at similar conclusions. His name is Patrick Harpur.

Just like Vallée and Mack, Harpur sees significance in the very absurdity and ambiguity of the calls of the absurd. Unlike Vallée's later writings, however, Harpur believes such characteristics to be natural – in fact, the most innate – attributes of these phenomena, not devices of premeditated Machiavellian deception. Harpur goes well beyond UFOs and alien abductions, classifying all kinds of visions and apparitions under what he calls 'daimonic reality.' (Here, the word 'daimonic' is not to be confused with the term 'demonic;' it does not have the same negative connotation.) In another similarity with the works of Vallée and Mack, Harpur discerns an 'intent' behind the calls of the absurd: he believes they are a spontaneous compensatory reaction to the very rationalist, materialist view of reality that discredits them to begin with.[14] This point of view is reminiscent of Jung's position on the role of dreams as purposeful compensatory reactions to unnatural psychic conditions.[15] Indeed, we will later see that dreams and the calls of the absurd may have much in common.

To Harpur, the calls of the absurd are protrusions into our consensus world of phenomena anchored in the daimonic realm: a realm that is both material and immaterial; both fact and fiction. Thus, 'daimonic reality' is a kind of intermediate realm between the physical and the spiritual, between the world and the imagination, embodying characteristics of both. Harpur identifies this realm with what Jung called the 'collective unconscious,' although Harpur – more explicitly than Jung – does not restrict the daimonic to the inside of our heads alone. In the realm of the daimonic, the imagination operates in its most natural form: through analogical – not literal – thinking; through metaphor, not causally-closed modeling. Indeed, Jung has suggested that parables and similes are an older, more archaic mode of thought than linear logic and rationality. This archaic mode of thinking currently survives mostly in dreams.[16]

Because of its defiance of any literal explanation and its inability to fit into any well-defined category, the daimonic is fundamentally elusive, ambiguous, shape-shifting.[17] It is these characteristics that led Harpur to identify the world of fairies – as captured in the folklore of Celtic traditions – as an archetypical example of daimonic reality. After all, fairies are morally ambiguous; their manifestation absurd, yet consistent across the ages.[18] Fairies – like UFOs, aliens, and DMT elves – are daimons. Vallée, as we have seen, had arrived decades earlier at similar conclusions.

Yet, the elusiveness of the daimonic does not imply its lack of physicality. Indeed, Harpur stresses that daimonic phenomena can have very physical effects, suggesting that the manifestation of these effects may be linked to what Jung called 'synchronistic events,'[19] which we briefly discussed earlier. However, the physical traces daimonic events leave behind are themselves just as ambiguous and elusive as the original phenomena. These traces can be construed to lend support to different – and mutually contradictory – attempts at explaining the phenomena. Hence, despite encompassing undeniable physical aspects, the calls of the absurd trick our logic and refuse to be boxed in or labeled unambiguously. Whatever we attempt to say they are, they show they are not; whatever we attempt to say they are not, they indicate they might just be.[20]

Harpur stresses that, from the point of view of the daimons, *their* reality is the true ground of existence, the world of ego-consciousness being merely a kind of dream consisting of projected images of what we conceive the daimonic to be.[21] He suggests that dreams and other non-ordinary states of consciousness offer us a door into the daimonic; a door we can use to explore a world operating under different rules, the experience of which may release us from certain ingrained and rusty patterns of thinking; a door that enables us to see through the literal appearances of the world we experience through ego-consciousness.[22] If we do not voluntarily open the door to the daimons, Harpur suggests that the daimons then force themselves into our world through the calls of the absurd. The daimons strive constantly to escape their exile in the unconscious, continuously challenging the literalism of our worldview.

Harpur is self-consistent in his approach to the calls of the absurd: because he believes them to represent a reality that transcends the explanatory power of logic and physics, he does not offer a direct explanation for them.[23] Instead, he takes an indirect approach in his books: by discussing different examples of calls of the absurd under the light of philosophy, esotericism, and even poetry, Harpur attempts to convey a roundabout impression – an intuitive way of seeing – that is conducive to the intellectual acceptance of the calls of the absurd without need for a closed, causal explanation. His work is quite remarkable in that he largely succeeds in this formidable and unusual challenge. Yet, it leaves readers with more rational and less poetic inclinations a little frustrated. I confess to be one such reader, for I asked myself after reading Harpur's work: Wonderful but, at the end of the day, just *what* is going on then? Just *what* are the calls of the absurd after all? No straight answer was to be found.

In this book, I set out to tackle precisely this gap: to suggest a direct and explicit *explanation* for phenomena that defy the very logic grounding such explanation. I will attempt this in the tradition of Kurt Gödel, who defeated an entire system of logical thought while operating *within* the very system whose defeat he achieved.[24] In the next chapter, we will start on the tricky road towards this elusive explanation. Since we will tackle the absurd initially from within the confines of logic and physics, some structured and disciplined thinking will be required of you. Bear with me, for later we will return to the absurd and place it within the framework of a surprising, yet well-founded, conception of reality.

Chapter 3

The demise of realism

A common characteristic of many interpretations of the absurd, as discussed in the previous chapter, is a blurring of the boundaries between the inner reality of the psyche and the outer reality of the physical world. Indeed, the alleged dichotomy between subjectivity and objectivity, which reigns supreme in our culture, seems to be the major stumbling block in any attempt to make sense of the phenomena I have referred to as 'calls of the absurd.' After all, if this alleged dichotomy were not framing our thinking, we would recognize mind and world to be essentially continuous with one another, so it would not be surprising at all that physicality is just as non-literal, symbolic, and metaphorical as our nightly dreams. But by separating world from mind, we have rendered this otherwise natural insight – which traditional cultures consider so self-evident that they fail to understand the distinction we make between literal and metaphorical – utterly unacceptable. Our culture has gotten away with this so far because, since the transition from the Renaissance to the Enlightenment in about the 17th or 18th century, we have simply chosen to ignore certain classes of phenomena in defining our mainstream worldview.

But before we continue with our reasoning, we must lay out some semantic foundations for the sake of clarity. I am speaking here of the qualifier 'objective,' which we tend to use in two different ways. Almost always these two different meanings are consistent with one another, so we do not even realize that we are saying two different things. But in the discussion that follows we will need to make that distinction explicit and clear.

We say that something is 'objective' when the thing observed is not the product of someone's individual imagination. If the thing is objective in this sense, then multiple observers will describe it in similar and consistent ways. Furthermore, this kind of objectivity entails that an individual observer is incapable of independently changing the reality of what is observed. For instance, an imaginary tree on the screen of someone's mind is not objective, for the person can change or destroy the tree at will simply by manipulating his or her own mental processes. Moreover, an imagined tree cannot be observed by multiple people. On the other hand, a physical tree in the garden is objective in this sense because, try as one might, the tree is still there even if one attempts to visualize something else in its place. This is the first sense in which we use the qualifier 'objective.' Let us call this 'weak-objectivity.' *Something is weakly-objective when it can be consistently observed by multiple individuals and when it cannot be independently altered by an individual act of cognition.*

The other quality we attribute to something by saying that it is 'objective' is its independence of conscious observation in general. Thus, if a meteorite can be said to have fallen in the middle of the remotest desert, even though no living creature has seen, heard, or otherwise perceived anything associated with the event, then we can say that the meteorite's fall is 'strongly-objective.' *Something is strongly-objective when its existence or occurrence is fundamentally independent of conscious observation.*

Note that weak-objectivity does *not* necessarily entail or imply strong-objectivity. Indeed, we have defined weak-objectivity in such a way that observation is always part of the equation. As such, one cannot talk of weak-objectivity at all unless there are at least two observers involved. Strong-objectivity, on the other hand, holds even when *no observers* are involved. The very definition of strong-objectivity requires that the existence of something can be inferred with certainty in the absence of any observation at all.

You may have to stretch your imagination a little to conceive of a thing or event that is weakly-objective while *not* being strongly-objective. So let us elaborate on this possibility with a thought exercise: imagine that a technology were invented that permitted human beings to share dreams. In other words, imagine a machine that enabled people to plug into each other's dreams. The experiences we shared in this way would still be a dream, taking place entirely in our minds and not in the outside world. But the dream-sharing machine would measure, communicate, and control all relevant mental processes in our minds while we slept, thereby harmonizing our dreams so we all had the same, collaboratively built experience. The events in these shared dreams would fit the definition of weak-objectivity: multiple observers would presumably describe the same events. Moreover, no individual dreamer would be able to independently manipulate those events, for the machine synchronizing the dreamers' mental patterns would continuously inject patterns from other dreamers into the picture. And yet, the dreamed events would obviously not fit the definition of strong-objectivity: without conscious dreamers, there would be no events. Performing this thought exercise a few times could help you develop an intuition for the difference between strong- and weak-objectivity, as well as gain insight into why the latter does not necessarily entail or imply the former.

Let us now use the semantic tool we have just constructed: to the extent that different and independent observers reported seeing the same thing, the Hessdalen lights, the Hudson valley UFO sightings, and the Miracle of the Sun at Fátima were all weakly-objective. To assert that a thing or event is strongly-objective, on the other hand, requires an inductive leap of faith. The reason is clear: stating that a thing or event exists or occurs in the absence of any observation of it is *always* a leap of faith. Here the usefulness of the distinction between weak- and strong-objectivity becomes very clear: we should be able to say *for sure* when something is objective in the weak sense, but without having to state at the same time that the thing exists independently of observation in general. Having made this distinction, *we can now say with certainty that weak-objectivity is a potential quality of calls of the absurd,* even though we cannot deduce strong-objectivity from it.

The inevitable question arising in anyone's mind upon reading Chapter 1 of this book is: 'Are these calls of the absurd *real*?' Because if they are not real, in the sense that they are delusional or mere fabrications, then this entire book is pointless. Above, we have answered half of this question: yes, calls of the absurd are real insofar as they are weakly-objective. In other words, they are real to the people who jointly witness them, and cannot be explained as individual delusions or fabrications. But we are now left with the other half of the question: Do these calls of the absurd exist outside mentation? Are they strongly-objective as well?

Any discussion about the strong-objectivity of calls of the absurd is secondary in view of a much broader question: *Is strong-objectivity a property that can be confidently attributed to any aspect of nature at all?* Can anything at all be said, with certainty, to be strongly-objective? This is a question that has been asked by thinkers since time immemorial. Much has been written about it. Therefore, to continue with our analysis properly, we must place it in a broader historical and philosophical context.

The notion of strong-objectivity corresponds to what is known in the philosophy of science as 'realism.'[1] Realism is a philosophy holding that nature is independent of cognition. According to realism, the facts of nature are all already 'out there' from the beginning, just waiting for human beings to discover them. Historically, realism has been contrasted with the philosophy of 'idealism,' which holds that the world is a construct of mind. Many scientists have an instinctive dislike of idealism, because it may seem to imply that scientific discoveries are not discoveries at all, but self-validating inventions of human cognition. Still, scientists themselves accept that all we can ever experience as human beings is bundles of sense data in our mind, never the external world where the sense data supposedly originate. We have no direct access to a supposedly external world and no way to prove its existence, for we are forever locked in the subjective space of our consciousness. Therefore, a mind-independent world remains an *assumption*, tempting as it may be.

What drives this temptation is the consistency with which different people seem to describe the world. After all, we all seem to agree on what the world looks like. For there to be such commonality of description, at least one of the following two hypotheses must hold: either (a) we are all observing the same strongly-objective world, or (b) our minds are fundamentally connected to one another so we can all share the same 'dream.' Now, because there is an empirical correlation between minds and brains, realists implicitly assume that brains generate minds. And since brains are clearly separate from one another, realists then argue that minds must also be separate from one another and hypothesis (b) must be discarded. All we are then left with is (a), thereby proving realism correct – or so the argument goes. There is, however, a fundamental flaw in this line of reasoning: it begs the question. In other words, for the argument to work, it must assume the very hypothesis it seeks to prove. Indeed, the idea that minds are circumscribed by brains entails realism to begin with, insofar as it assumes that brains are discrete mind-independent objects in the world that, in turn, generate minds. But if realism is *not* true, then brains must themselves be constructs *of* mind, *in* mind; not the other way around. In this case, the fact that different brains are separate from each other says nothing about the possibility that minds are connected or even unitary. As such, hypothesis (b) cannot be discarded. The entire argument for realism thus falls apart and, once again, we see that consistency of description can only be construed as evidence for weak-objectivity, not realism. For all we know, we may all be having a shared 'dream.'

These brief considerations should illustrate why idealism is considered a serious philosophical position. It is a position that has been taken and defended by a great number of highly respected thinkers. People of the caliber of George Berkeley, Immanuel Kant, Georg Hegel, Gottfried Leibniz, and John McTaggart, among many others, have all argued persuasively for different forms of idealism. In a way, what is surprising is that idealism is considered so fringe and improbable by society at large.

Perhaps it is modern cultural biases that make it so hard for us to accept the idea that the world we live in may be a construct of mind. How could mind alone create an entire universe and then experience this universe as if it were living inside it? How could mind experience itself as if it were something external to itself? All valid questions. Yet, every night we are given an incontrovertible demonstration of the power of mind to do just that: when we dream, our mind creates rich, apparently externalized worlds so it can experience itself as if it were split into subject and objects. In a dream, mind inhabits itself. Dreams, while we are in them, are wholly indistinguishable from physical reality. I once tested this assertion to convince myself of it: during a lucid dream, while fully cognizant that I was asleep, I looked around the world created by my own mind and asked myself whether it was distinguishable from my ordinary waking world in terms of its level of detail, clarity, or of how convincing it felt to me. The answer was an unambiguous 'no.' I just could not tell the difference. Is it thus so hard to imagine that I may be 'dreaming' as I write these words, and that you may be 'dreaming' as you read this book?

As discussed earlier, there is no direct empirical way to prove idealism wrong or realism right. For many scientists and philosophers, this renders the metaphysical debate around the clash 'realism versus idealism' uninteresting, despite the tremendous importance it clearly carries in shaping our view of reality. Therefore, and considering the turn toward pragmatism that our culture took in the second half of the 20th century, the debate has now moved on to the clash 'realism versus anti-realism.'

Unlike idealism, anti-realism makes no metaphysical assertions about the nature of reality. That is, it stops short of claiming that the world is fundamentally a construct of mind. Instead, it focuses solely on limiting the ontological assertions that can be derived from scientific theories. It seeks to restrict the scope of the conclusions that can be extracted from the practical, empirical success of science. According to anti-realism, scientifically postulated entities that cannot be observed directly – like subatomic particles – are just *metaphors*; *myths* that help us explain and predict natural phenomena. They do not necessarily shed any light on the fundamental nature of what is really going on. An anti-realist would say that the concept of this or that subatomic particle is a useful one in that nature behaves *as if* there were such subatomic particles; but that does not at all mean that they *literally* exist and have the *literal* properties we attribute to them. Like the calls of the absurd, they are just metaphorical 'stories,' 'tales' we tell ourselves in our quest to find closure.

One of the key motivations for anti-realism is that most scientific theories 'underdetermine' the phenomena we observe. In other words, for any one observation we make, there are potentially many different 'stories' and 'invisible entities' that could successfully explain the observation. So the fact that a theory is successful in predicting observations does not necessarily mean that the theory is 'even roughly on the right lines'[2] as far as ontology is concerned. There are plenty of historical examples of empirically successful theories that have been proven wrong at a later time.[3]

Although the worldview of the majority of people today, scientists and laymen alike, entails the belief that the world exists 'out there,' independent of mind, this is but one alternative. The other alternative, idealism, has never been defeated as the basis for a viable worldview. In fact, idealism is a much more parsimonious alternative, for it makes no assumptions beyond acknowledging the existence of *experience*, the one undeniable truth about reality. Moreover, even if one refrains from taking a metaphysical position, anti-realism shows us that our realist models of nature are just *metaphors*. They are useful in practice for predicting the behavior of nature, but they should not be over-interpreted as providing us with a *literal* ontology of the world. *We base the entire edifice of our realist, materialist worldview on a foundation that, just like the calls of the absurd, is fundamentally metaphorical.* The implications of this are shattering. And yet we, as a civilization, insist on going about our business in blissful and willful ignorance of these questions.

So where does this leave us? Adopting an idealist worldview would certainly help us make sense of the calls of the absurd: their simultaneously physical and psychological reality would cease to be a problem, for what we call 'physical' would then be just a special modality of mental imagery. The physical world itself would be mental in essence, akin to a collective 'dream.' As such, nobody would take it literally, in the same way that nobody takes dreams literally. All aspects of the physical world would be symbolic: some logically so, some absurdly so, much like dreams can have both logical and absurd elements in their storylines.

But let us be honest with ourselves: realism is so deeply ingrained in our mind that we cannot discard it based solely on the limited, intrinsically elusive and contradictory evidence gathered from the calls of the absurd. We need much more substantial evidence for taking a position that defies the current cultural paradigm so dramatically.

As it turns out, this substantial evidence does exist. In fact, it is somewhat of a mystery why society is not abuzz with commotion about the dumbfounding implications of it. The evidence comes from experiments with so-called entangled subatomic particles. Because our world is supposedly made of subatomic particles, experiments on these tiny building blocks of nature actually inform us about the structure of our whole universe.

The experimental arrangement normally used is illustrated in Figure 1. A pair of two subatomic particles is simultaneously generated at a source and then sent out in opposite directions. The source can be, for instance, a light emitter, so that the pair of particles consists of two photons: one emitted towards the right, the other towards the left of the source. On either side, and at a sufficiently long distance from the source, a detector is placed that can measure a certain property of the incoming photon once it arrives.[4] Each detector can measure a different property of the respective incoming photon.[5] It takes some time for each photon to arrive at its respective detector. The distance between the source – in the middle – and each detector is to ensure that the measurement performed on one side cannot influence the measurement performed on the other side. In other words, we wait until the photons are far enough away from one another that they can be considered completely separated. Once this condition is fulfilled, we make a separate measurement of each photon, using the respective detector.

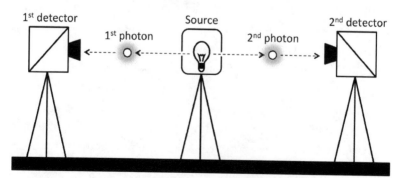

Figure 1. Caricature of a typical experimental arrangement for studying quantum entanglement

Now here comes the weirdness. The theory of quantum mechanics does not allow us to speak of the reality of the photons' properties prior to measuring them. So we must think in terms of the photons taking on the property to be measured[6] only at the moment of measurement, not at the moment of their emission from the source. Quantum mechanics also predicts that, whatever property the first photon 'chooses' to take on when measured by the first detector,[7] the property the second photon takes on when measured by the second detector will depend on the first photon's 'choice.'[8] Consequently, the *independent* measurements made by the two detectors are predicted to be strongly correlated with each other, despite their physical separation, such correlation depending on what specific combination of properties the detectors are configured to measure.[9] That is why we say that the photons are 'entangled.' At first sight, it is either as though the photons were still connected after they are emitted from the source, influencing each other's properties 'on the fly,' or as though the measured correlations were themselves not separate from the act of measurement, observation somehow causing the photons' properties to pop into existence. To early 20th-century physicists, this sounded like some kind of magic. Yet, as it turns out, early measurements confirmed these weird predictions of quantum mechanics.

During the first half of the 20th century, Danish physicist Niels Bohr – one of the fathers of quantum mechanics – intensely debated with Albert Einstein the implications of this result. In fact, they had fundamental disagreements about what to make of it. Einstein and his collaborators thought the experiments could be explained in another way: In addition to the properties that can be measured by the detectors, they postulated that the photons can have other, 'hidden properties.'[10] Moreover, they postulated that both photons in an entangled pair share an identical hidden property from the moment they are jointly created in the source, preserving it after they are emitted in opposite directions. It is this common hidden property that supposedly influences the measurements on both sides and explains the correlation between the independent observations at the two detectors. This way, the origin of the measurement correlation is supposedly the moment when the photons are created at the source (for then they are together and can influence one another), not the moment of measurement (when they are already physically separated from each other). Such explanation, if correct, would dispense with the need for the photons in an entangled pair to be still 'spookily connected' to one another at the moment of measurement, or for their properties to be 'magically' determined by the very act of observation. Note, however, that Einstein did not elaborate on what these hidden properties were or how they worked; he simply pointed out that they were conceivable.

Einstein's hypothesis above is the basis for what is currently called – for obvious reasons – the 'hidden variables' theories of quantum entanglement. According to these theories, the entangled photons do not influence one another at a distance, but simply share a hidden property from the beginning; the photons' properties are not 'brought into being' by observation, but are fully determined from the moment of the photons' creation. The correlations observed between measurements done on different photons simply reflect the commonality of a hypothetical hidden property that both photons have from the get-go.

Notice that Einstein's view was grounded in *realism*: the hypothetical hidden properties are seen as facts of the world 'out there,' completely independent of observation. In other words, the hidden properties are assumed to be strongly-objective. Moreover, Einstein's view also assumes *locality*: the hidden property of each entangled photon resides solely in the respective photon and depends on nothing outside it, even if the hidden property happens to be the same in both photons of the pair. Because of these two characteristics, we say that these hidden variables theories of quantum entanglement entail *local realism.* More importantly, *local realism requires a hidden variables theory of quantum entanglement to hold true.* If not, local realism is fallacious. In this latter case, the question would then be: Which part of local realism has to be abandoned? Locality, realism, or both?

As it turns out, some of the early measurements on entangled photons could conceivably be explained, in principle, by strongly-objective, hypothetical hidden properties shared by the two photons from the moment of their joint creation. But the question remained: Could hidden variables *always* explain the predictions of quantum mechanics in *all* situations?

Decades later, in the 1960s, physicist John Bell entered the fray.[11] What he did was to carefully work out the statistical implications of Einstein's local-realist views. Bell was able to contrast the theoretical predictions of quantum mechanics with the explanatory power of *any* local hidden variables theory for a whole range of experimental scenarios, not just a handful. More specifically, Bell looked at all combinations of properties the pair of detectors could be configured to measure, and determined that for many of these combinations quantum mechanics made predictions that deviated from what could be expected from any local hidden variables theory.[12] He could then theoretically prove that *no local hidden variables theory could match quantum mechanical predictions for all situations.* There were clear differences between what local-realist hidden properties could conceivably explain and what quantum mechanics predicted. Therefore, one of the two had to be wrong.

The consequence of Bell's work was that the philosophical debate between Einstein and Bohr could then, for the first time, be translated into an *empirical* question. One could, in principle, construct an experimental setup to test entanglement under conditions for which Bell demonstrated that quantum mechanics would predict results that local-realist hidden properties could not possibly explain. In practice, however, it was very difficult and expensive to perform these tests: they required highly sophisticated apparatuses, as well as extremely delicate and subtle experimental procedures. Not until the early 1980s were sufficiently reliable tests performed under Bell's conditions.

The first of these tests were those performed by Alain Aspect and his team in 1981 and '82, in France.[13] In his tests, Aspect placed the detectors at a 6-meter distance from the photon source in the middle, so the two detectors stood at a 12-meter distance from one another. This ensured good separation between the measurements performed with each respective detector. Aspect's progressively more elaborate and accurate experiments showed a clear violation of the explanatory limits of local-realist hidden properties, as well as a clear agreement with quantum mechanical predictions. It appeared that local realism was dead.

Still, critics were able to point out a few potential loopholes in the experimental setup. One way to increase the reliability of the conclusions was to perform new tests with an increased distance between the detectors. The intent was to reduce the already remote likelihood that the measured correlations could be explained by a lack of sufficient physical separation between the measurements taking place on each side. Following this approach, a 1998 experiment done in Geneva, Switzerland, innovated by injecting the photons of an entangled pair into the optical fibers of a commercial telecommunications network.[14] This allowed the scientists to increase the distance between the detectors to *several kilometers*, instead of the few meters used in Aspect's original experiments. Again, the measured correlations confirmed the predictions of quantum mechanics and exceeded the envelope of what local-realist hidden variables could explain.

But skeptics were not yet defeated. They postulated another loophole: that the two detectors could perhaps be exchanging – *in advance of the photon emissions* – some kind of signal that could influence the correlations measured. In other words – and far-fetched as it may sound – the idea was that the detectors might be 'tipping each other off' in advance. Alternatively – but just as implausible – perhaps the detectors could be tipping the source off: if the source somehow 'knew,' in advance, the precise combination of properties the pair of detectors was configured to measure, it could conceivably generate photons with the exact hidden property necessary to cause the expected correlations. The hypothesis borders on ludicrousness, but anyway...

Notice that what was on the table here was not a coherent and complete proposal for how this 'tipping off' might operate. No concrete mechanisms of action were hypothesized. Instead, the argument was merely a kind of placeholder: a speculation that *there could conceivably be something going on* to link the detectors and the source, whatever that something might be. Clearly, it was becoming increasingly precarious to find ways to dismiss the evidence. But scientists pressed on in their judicious quest to eliminate every conceivable loophole.

So in that same year of 1998, but this time in Innsbruck, Austria, a test was done[15] with a crucial twist: the detectors were each time reconfigured *after the photons had already left the source*. In other words, the photons were already in flight when the system selected what property each detector was to measure.[16] Moreover, the selection was automated and random, so nobody knew it in advance. The scientists thus eliminated the loophole: there was not enough time for any communication to take place between the detectors, or between a detector and the source, once the detectors 'knew' what property they were supposed to measure. There was not enough time for the detectors to tip each other off, or tip the source off, about what they were going to do. The setup was so elegant that Alain Aspect considered it 'ideal.'[17] The results of the experiment, as you might be expecting by now, were once again in excellent agreement with the predictions of quantum mechanics and in defiance of the possibilities of local-realist hidden variables.

As highlighted by Alain Aspect,[18] there is a further, fascinating facet to this experiment: as soon as one of the detectors was reconfigured, a change in the correlations observed in the other detector would become *instantaneously* apparent, without any delay that could accommodate hypothetical signal propagation between the detectors. So how did the photons arriving at the other detector 'know' instantly, on the fly, that the configuration of the first detector, placed far away, had been changed? No local-realist hidden variables theory could account for this. It seemed to imply either that entangled particles are fundamentally inseparable, despite physical distance, or that the very act of observation somehow plays into the reality of the experiment and creates the correlations. Either alternative is paradigm-shattering for the reigning worldview of our culture.

Clearly, something had to give. For most scientists, it was much easier to give up locality than realism, so embedded is realism into the scientific way of thinking. The majority, therefore, chose to interpret the results discussed above as evidence that particles are fundamentally connected to one another beyond space-time limitations; that nature must be studied as a unified whole, not as a collection of separate parts. To accommodate and substantiate this choice, scientists proposed *non*-local hidden variables theories of quantum entanglement.

Non-local hidden variables theories part with the idea that the hypothetical hidden properties reside exclusively in the particles themselves. They postulate, instead, that the hidden properties are 'smeared out' in space-time in a non-local manner. Nonetheless, the hidden properties remain part of the world 'out there,' strongly-objective and independent of mind or observation. Realism could thus be preserved by these theories, even though they necessitated a weird take on the nature of the hidden properties. That is why a paper published in 2007, in *Nature* – likely the most respected peer-reviewed scientific periodical in the world – is so important.[19]

The paper describes a theoretical and experimental analysis

performed by a team of Austrian and Polish physicists. The team identified a set of previously untested correlations between entangled photons that, if confirmed experimentally, would rule out a significant class of theories based on *non*-local hidden properties. Sure enough, the correlations were confirmed. The team's conclusion was that abandoning locality is not enough to explain quantum entanglement: *one needs to abandon realism itself;* or at least some very intuitive features of realism. But if these intuitive features are dropped, one must then ask whether it still makes sense to use the word 'realism.'

The bottom line is: the results of the 2007 analysis and experiments make the standard intuitions behind the notion of realism untenable. *It is thus fair to say, within the current framework of scientific thought, that realism as we normally understand it must be abandoned.* Remember, the inconceivably small subatomic particles these experiments are performed on are supposedly building blocks of the whole of nature. Therefore, the defeat of realism for subatomic particles entails that *there is no such a thing as a strongly-objective world.* This is a shattering and most significant conclusion for most people's outlook on reality. Yet, and somewhat frustratingly, it is hardly discussed outside highly specialized circles.

The evidence does not restrict itself to pairs of subatomic particles: correlations between states of mind and of the physical world have been found through experiments focusing on large world events. The Global Consciousness Project (GCP) – started at the Engineering Anomalies Research Laboratory at Princeton University in the early 1990s – has shown significant correlation between human mental activity associated with global events and the outputs of random number generators.[20] These generators are electronic coin-flippers: normally, over a long enough period, one would expect them to output roughly the same number of heads and tails. But at around the time of events causing major emotional upheaval in large populations – like the 9/11 terrorist attacks[21] or the burial of Princess Diana – the results have shown marked and sustained trends towards either heads or tails. Having carried out 280 tests under stringent conditions, over a 10-year period, the GCP team has found a correlation between mental states and physical events whose odds against chance are 1 to 20 million. As Princeton Professor Roger Nelson put it, 'we don't yet know how to explain the correlations between events of importance to humans and the GCP data, but they are quite clear.'[22] One must keep in mind that this is a statistical result; but then again, all empirical, scientific conclusions are derived from significant-enough statistics. The result does seem to indicate that mental states (the global emotional outpouring accompanying major world events) and physical reality (the output of random number generators placed across the globe) are not separate. In other words, realism is again challenged by hard-nosed empirical observations.

Although it is the mainstream view in science today that local hidden variables theories have failed, and that local realism has been defeated, a few influential scientists still insist on versions of it.[23] As an engineer, I am not sufficiently qualified to judge the merits of these proposals on their technical content. But it does strike me that a paradigm of thought clearly does not concede ground easily, even in light of what apparently can be considered overwhelming evidence (we will look at this peculiar and historical phenomenon in more detail in a later chapter). To save some form of a hidden variables theory of entanglement, other scientists have come up with what could be considered quite weird alternatives. For instance, scenarios have been devised where signals travel back in time to construct the measured correlations without violating relativity theory's speed-of-light limit.[24] One cannot help but wonder which alternative sounds more mythical and fairytale-like: idealism or quantum histories arriving *en masse* from the future. Either way, as far as weirdness is concerned, the scientific *status quo* does make the calls of the absurd sound somewhat more docile in comparison.

The weirdness of entanglement and of other experimentally verified aspects of quantum mechanics has led to a proliferation of hypotheses about the nature of reality that rival the most outrageous science fiction novels: parallel worlds, hyper-dimensional multiverses, simulated realities, time travel, and many other ideas that are beyond the realm of empirical verification. The people proposing these fantastic ideas are impossible to ignore: they include some of our best scientists. In a way – and I run the risk of being unfair in my judgment here – these proposals represent a psychological trade-off: one knows that some weirdness is unavoidable, so one carefully cherry-picks which weirdness to let in, so as to preserve the aspect of one's personal worldview that is psychologically most difficult to abandon. For some, realism must be preserved at all costs; for others, determinism; for yet others, locality. So selecting among these theories becomes largely a matter of *taste*. Now, personally – and this may come as a surprise to you at this point – *I have nothing at all against it*. I believe this kind of scientific open-mindedness and imagination – biased as it may be – is essential to the evolution of our understanding of reality. That said, I also think that we must maintain perspective: for now, these 'theories' are just stories. In stating this, some of the arguments of physicist Lee Smolin against String Theory come to my mind.[25]

As it will later become clear, if the ideas articulated in this book have any validity, story-making is more than just acceptable: it is essential. I believe we must keep on creating myths – scientific and otherwise – for these myths may be the color and substance of life and the world. But by taking any one of these myths as the *literal truth*, one takes a heavy burden upon oneself. If we choose one and close our mind to all the other metaphors of reality – to all the other myths – we may find our life impoverished and meaningless. We may fail to see the richness and significance of Joe Simonton's unsalted pancakes and of centuries of fairy lore. When we read a fairy tale, we may see only silliness. When we look at the van Gogh the world is, we may see only grays. We become blind to our own dreams and forget them every morning. But then again, this book is itself just a story; a myth that, by operation of the very ideas it articulates, negates itself like the calls of the absurd.

One may have reservations about the open-mindedness embodied in all the new and weird myths currently proliferating in physics. But the opposite attitude is a lot more pernicious and dangerous: *apathy in face of the crumbling of a reigning worldview.* Even among thinkers who accept that the current worldview is untenable, there seems to be a kind of cognitive split going on: yes, they acknowledge the failure of the old paradigm, but they go on with their work and outlook as if nothing had changed. There is no concerted effort in society today to try and articulate the remarkable implications of the defeat of the present, culturally sanctioned worldview. Were that to be done, it would change how we see the world, how we do science, how we educate our children and, ultimately, how we live our lives. *This* is the real shame, for it turns our culture into a fossil; into a hardened shell that imprisons the imagination like an arthropod unable to molt.

All we can assert about the reality of *anything* is its weak-objectivity. Only for weak-objectivity are there clear criteria for making such assertions. Based on these criteria, we can state that calls of the absurd are weakly-objective, and this is as much as can be said of anything: stars, mountains, chairs, photons, and history. Calls of the absurd cannot be asserted to be strongly-objective. But then again, *nothing* can be asserted to be strongly-objective; not only because there are no direct criteria for making such assertion, but because – as we have just seen – an overwhelming and still growing amount of scientific evidence indicates that strong-objectivity is but an abstract figment of our conceptual imagination. Therefore, calls of the absurd are as real as anything. They are as much an inherent part of our condition as the consensus world surrounding us.

It is ironic that science, through the diligent and consequent pursuit of a materialist, strongly-objective view of nature, would lead to the very evidence that renders such view untenable. As we will later see, it is a recurring theme in different branches of science and philosophy that the pursuit of a rational system of thought ultimately leads to its own defeat. There is something perennial about the idea that any *literal* view of nature, when pursued to its ultimate ramifications, destroys itself from within. It is as though every literal model carried within itself the seeds of its own falsification; as if nature resisted attempts to be limited or otherwise boxed in. Whatever we say it is, it indicates it is not; whatever we say it is not, it shows it might just be. These are built-in mechanisms of growth and renewal in nature that we ignore at our own peril. Nature is as fluid and elusive as a thought. Indeed, it *is* a thought: an unfathomable, compound thought we live in and contribute to. *The world is a shared 'dream.' In it, as in a regular dream, the dreamer is himself the subject and the object; the observer and the observed.*

Chapter 4

The desacralization of logic

As we have seen in the previous chapter, scientific evidence indicates that the world is fundamentally inseparable from our subjective mental picture of it; much like a shared, collective 'dream.' Strong-objectivity appears to be fallacious and the 'subject versus object' duality a mere illusion. Naturally, two sets of questions then immediately arise, which I would like to acknowledge upfront: First, if the world is really akin to a dream, how come it is so seemingly autonomous? How come we wake up every day to where the world has gone – apparently without us – since we last fell asleep? And if it is the minds of countless different individuals that help make up the 'dream,' how come it is so consistent – that is, weakly-objective? I dwelled on these questions in my previous work.[1] An idea discussed there was that a perfectly consistent and seemingly autonomous world would *inevitably* and *naturally* emerge, by itself, if individual minds could communicate within the 'dream.' Now, the second set of questions may be even more disconcerting for the casual idealist: There is a strong and undeniable correlation between states of mind and states of the brain. The idealist notion that mind creates brain easily accommodates this correlation. Yet, if it is indeed the mind that creates the brain, as opposed to the other way around, how come we seem to lose (a memory of) consciousness when anesthetized? How come our mind feels different when we add alcohol to the chemistry of the brain? Again, I dwelled on these questions in another earlier work.[2] The idea there was that both alcohol and brain are, ultimately, images of mental processes, which can thus influence one another. The brain is the image of a space-time localization of mind; a kind of anchor that allows a 'dreamer' to take a specific vantage point within the 'dream' and act as a character within it (in much the same way that, when we dream at night, we have dreamed-up bodies that anchor a localized vantage point within the dream). This locality anchor may work like a filter of perception: when the filter is disturbed within the context of the 'dream,' our perceptions within the 'dream' are themselves disturbed.

We will touch on these questions again later, but I hope to have given you an intuition about possible answers, as well as some references for further reading. The important point facing us now is the following: Whether we can articulate a coherent version of idealism or not, we are still left with the likely defeat of realism arising from hard science, as we have seen in the previous chapter. The implications of that alone are formidable and may require a fundamental revision of everything we believe to know about the world and ourselves. Even the most sacred foundation of our thinking may need to be revised: *logic itself.*

Every one of us, knowingly or unknowingly, holds many things to be true. Typically, we organize our 'truths' on different levels, according to how open to revising or reconsidering them we feel. For instance, we may hold certain opinions to be true about the state of our country's economy, though we know full well that we may be wrong about it. On another level, we may be fairly confident that the laws of physics we learned at school are true, though we know that occasionally they are also revised. However, at the most fundamental level, we draw an epistemic line: *logic* itself must be unquestionably, irrefutably true. If there is anything in existence that is conclusively, eternally, and self-evidently valid, it must be the laws of logic. We can tolerate changes in the 'truths' of economics, sociology, biology, and even physics, but not logic. Logic is sacred – or so the intuition goes.

Our unquestioned faith in logic is, in principle, somewhat problematic. As the skeptic Greek philosopher Agrippa argued centuries ago in his famous 'Trilemma,' we cannot use logic to justify the validity of logic itself. Agrippa's Trilemma, in more elaborate and modern forms, continues to be argued by contemporary philosophers.[3] A conclusion of the argument is that logic is itself grounded in illogical foundations and that we, strictly speaking, cannot rule out the possibility that existence is governed by absurdity. Yet, despite our inability to rationally justify logic, we have a powerful, innate intuition that logic is *self-evident* and *does not require justification* (I admit to suffering from a particularly severe form of this condition). As Prof. Graham Priest once wondered, 'Are the rules of logic hard-wired into us?'[4]

It is at least uncomfortable that the foundations of our rationality seem ultimately held together by vague intuition alone. As Douglas Hofstadter put it in his book *Gödel, Escher, Bach*, when writing about the difficulty of using logic to defend logic, 'At some point, you reach rock bottom, and there is no defense except loudly shouting, "I know I'm right!" ... you can't go on defending your patterns of reasoning forever. There comes a point where *faith* takes over'[5] (emphasis added). Oxford Professor Sir Roger Penrose once went as far as beginning one of his books by proposing that logical truths, as reflected in mathematics, belong to a 'Platonic world of absolutes.'[6] He then stated that he thinks of the physical world 'as emerging out of' this platonic world of absolutes.[7] It could be argued that Penrose's views elevate logic to a transcendent level in some ways analogous to mystical or religious truth. To be fair, however, Penrose simply had the courage to explicitly articulate what most of us in science and philosophy assume implicitly. Indeed, since the Age of Enlightenment, *our culture has sacralized logic*.

But let us not go too far here. Logic has an undeniable thing going for it: *when applied in practice, it always seems to work*. An idealist would argue that, since the world is fundamentally a projection of the mind, the empirical success of something we all believe in so viscerally and unreservedly, such as logic, is hardly a surprise. Nonetheless, the consistency between logic and empirical observation is too overwhelming for us to abandon logic based purely on a skeptical argument such as Agrippa's Trilemma. My intent in bringing the Trilemma into this discussion was simply to point out that the validity of logic should, in principle, not be so easily taken for granted as we tend to do.

Now, the real question I want to tackle is: If the experimental verification of quantum entanglement has indeed defeated realism, what are the implications for our ability to think logically about reality? What assumptions behind what we call 'logical thinking' may we need to revise? Indeed, *the realist worldview has shaped the rules of our current logic.* Much of what we intuitively think of as 'self-evident logical truths' is, to a surprising extent, determined implicitly by the assumption of realism; that is, by the assumption that the world 'out there' is strongly-objective and exists independently of our cognition. Below, we will review how this is so. Later in this chapter, we will discuss why a switch to idealism would force us to revise our logic.

The discussion in earlier chapters has focused on attempts to make sense of the phenomena of nature. This way, the questions raised have taken the following form: 'How does this or that phenomenon work?' Naturally, we can also transpose the same discussion onto a different form: we can reframe it in terms of questions about the truth or falsity of certain statements. For instance, we may ask: 'Is it true that entangled particles are connected beyond space-time limitations?' Or 'Is it true that aliens and fairies exist?' When reframing our epistemology – that is, our knowledge of the world – in terms of truth statements, we lose no generality.

Now, according to realism, every question of the form 'Is it true that ...?' must have a definite and unambiguous answer anchored in the facts of the physical world 'out there;' such facts being independent of our cognition. In other words, any proposition about the world is either true or false depending on the strongly-objective fact(s) it refers to, even if we do not know which one is the correct answer. For instance, the proposition 'Something large fell from the sky at Fátima in 1917' is linked to the strongly-objective event of an object falling from the sky. If the object existed and did fall from the sky, the proposition is true; otherwise, it is false. To the realist, whether we know the correct answer or not changes nothing about the fact that one, and only one, of the two possibilities (true or false) is the correct one, for the answer is always anchored in neutral facts outside mentation. This is often referred to as the 'correspondence theory of truth.'

It is this realism-inspired anchoring of all truth statements in (supposedly) strongly-objective facts that has found its way into logic as the 'principle of bivalence.' As Prof. Stephen Read put it, 'By linking the condition of truth of a proposition to a corresponding object – the fact – we are naturally led to Bivalence – either the proposition is true (for there is a fact corresponding to it) or it is false (for there is no such object). Hence every proposition is either true or false – and is so, regardless of our ability to discover it.'[8] Indeed, this sounds very logical to the vast majority of people. Would you not think it 'self-evidently true' that any statement about a fact of the world must be either true or false, depending on that stubborn fact? This does not seem to require any justification; it is obvious on the face of it – or so our realism-inspired logic goes.

The principle of bivalence is at the core of logic. It is this principle that motivates a definite, clear-cut worldview wherein ambiguity is not allowed. To put it in a different way, the principle of bivalence forces on us a *literal reality*: things and phenomena have one, and only one, correct explanation. Anything other than that explanation is just a subjective, and ultimately false, construct of the brain. Joe Simonton either literally saw three space travelers from another civilization – scoring a few unsalted pancakes in the process – or he did not; his experience was either literally true or literally false. Jim Sparks was either literally abducted by space aliens or literally delusional; there is no middle ground. This is the legacy of the principle of bivalence in how we think logically about the world. And, through the correspondence theory of truth, it is entirely motivated by a realist conception of nature.

To be fair, things are not quite as black and white as I have painted them above. Logic does produce some paradoxes and ambiguities. But these tend to be language paradoxes that are often dismissed as mere semantic quirks, bearing no relevance to the empirical world 'out there.' In other words, they are seen as mere artifacts of the tool – language – we use to describe the world, not of the world itself. Yet, if realism is fallacious, language paradoxes can no longer be inconsequentially dismissed, for 'semantic quirks' will then be inextricably linked to the world. Let us look at these paradoxes now.

Perhaps the simplest and clearest of semantic paradoxes is the so-called Liar Paradox. Here is a short version of it:

This statement is not true.

Now consider it for a moment. According to the principle of bivalence, we have two possibilities: either the statement above is true or it is false. Suppose that the statement is indeed true. Then what it says of itself is true, meaning that it must be false. But if the statement is false, then what it says of itself is false, meaning that it must be true. Whether you initially assume the statement to be true or false, the assumption immediately backfires and forces you to its opposite. So we are left with the conclusion that the statement must be *true and false at the same time*. Moreover, if you keep on playing this game, you will find yourself returning again and again to the assumption you started with, as in a closed loop. So the concurrent truth and falsity of the statement are organized according to what Hofstadter has called a 'strange loop.'[9] Like the calls of the absurd, semantic paradoxes are slippery: however you try to interpret them, they show you that the opposite interpretation must hold; whenever you try to pin their meaning down, its opposite springs forth; whatever literal conclusion you attempt to extract from them, another conclusion forces its way into your mind. Paradoxes are only whole when incorporating opposites as integral parts of the 'strange loop' they form.

Philosophers have tried for decades – if not centuries – to find the 'trick' behind this apparent absurdity, so as to show that there is actually no paradox here.[10] Yet, many attempts at 'resolving' the semantic paradoxes have failed. An approach in philosophy today is simply to bite the bullet and acknowledge the contradictions. As Prof. Stephen Read put it, the idea is 'to claim that what the paradoxes show is just what they seem to show – that certain contradictions must be accepted. Certain propositions really are paradoxical. *They really are both true and false*'[11] (emphasis added). Indeed, this position has been beautifully articulated and defended by Prof. Graham Priest in his book *In Contradiction*.[12] Prof. Priest's book is the quintessential work on 'dialetheism,' the view that there are true contradictions at least as far as language constructs go.

The existence of truly self-contradictory propositions – that is, of statements that are both true and false simultaneously – may be a tough pill to swallow for the rationalist. Therefore, you may find solace in the fact that we are talking 'merely' about the limitations of language constructs here, not the hard facts of nature in and of themselves. But not so fast: there is an inherent link between the structures of language[13] and how we construct our views and beliefs about the world.[14] Particularly, when we reflect abstractly upon what reality is and how it is put together, language constructs become largely co-extensive with our abstractions. In other words, we often tell ourselves *in language* what our views and beliefs about the world are. Therefore, *our worldviews may contain semantic paradoxes inherited from the way we articulate our views and beliefs to ourselves, using language structures.* This is a significant observation in light of the fact that, as we have seen in the previous chapter, the world appears to be inseparable from our subjective apprehension of it. Could semantic paradoxes then permeate the world itself? Could Jung's cave of the unconscious have been, paradoxically, *both* real and a mere fantasy? Could the roadside elves of our DMT study volunteer be trying to tell him something *simultaneously* real and delusional? Could the Hessdalen lights be *both* measurable and projected expectations?

Here is another thing to consider: paradoxes arise from self-reference.[15] It is by referring to themselves that paradoxical statements close the 'strange loop.' The semantic paradox considered above arose from the fact that a statement referred to its own untruthfulness. In that example, this was obvious. However, there are other paradoxes where the self-reference is more subtle, taking place indirectly. For instance, consider the following two statements:

The following statement is true.
The preceding statement is not true.

Again, a paradox arises. If the first statement is true, then it entails that the second statement is true; but the second statement entails that the first must be false. A similar contradiction arises if you initially consider the first statement false. You can check it for yourself. Here we again have a paradox arising from self-reference. However, this time the self-reference is indirect: the first statement refers ultimately to itself, but *through* the second statement; and vice-versa. The 'strange loop' is only closed across the two statements. We say that there is a 'layer of indirection' in the self-reference. There are other, much more convoluted paradoxes where there are so many layers of indirection that it is nearly impossible to find the self-reference – that is, the place where the 'strange loop' closes. Yet it is always there. As Hofstadter asked rhetorically, 'There seems to be one common culprit in these paradoxes, namely self-reference ... So if the goal is to ban all paradoxes, why not try banning self-reference and anything that allows it to arise?'[16]

But here is the problem: *If realism is false, nature is fundamentally self-referential in the sense that subject and object are not distinct.* When you look out at the world 'out there,' you may actually be looking at your own cognitive processes at work. When you defend propositions about the world you cognize around yourself, you may ultimately be defending propositions about propositions, just as in the semantic paradoxes above. Semantic paradoxes may be built into the very fabric of the world, but the self-reference of this process may be so deeply buried in layer upon layer of indirection that we almost never become cognizant of it in our daily lives. It may have become nearly impossible to see where the 'strange loop' of the world closes. These considerations provide reason to take seriously the possibility that the world is inherently vulnerable to paradox and contradiction, just like the semantics of language.

It may be hard for you to take to heart the idea that a few funny language games, when mixed in with some impenetrable laboratory experiments, can lead to the flabbergasting conclusion that the fabric of the world may have paradox woven into it. Yet, philosophers take these 'language games'[17] very seriously. To impress upon you that this is by no means mere philosophical hairsplitting, let us look at one of the most important results in the history of mathematics, which was derived from somewhat analogous considerations: Kurt Gödel's Incompleteness Theorems.

What Austrian logician Kurt Gödel did in 1931 was to prove

that the very same kind of contradiction found in the statement 'This statement is not true' lies at the core of number theory, the foundation of mathematics.[18] Gödel showed that self-reference is integral to number theory. Because of it, from a *literal* perspective, number theory is fundamentally limited: there are always true statements about numbers that cannot be derived from number theory, unless one accepts contradiction along with them. In other words, it is a fundamental limitation of mathematics that, try as we might, we can *never* know the whole truth about numbers while keeping absurdity at bay. *To know all there is to be known about numbers entails the embrace of paradox*, for it is integral to the 'strange loop' of mathematical theory. 'Why is this so relevant?' you might ask. Well, simply consider the fact that *the description of the world constructed by our physics is an edifice of numbers*. Pause for a moment and reflect upon this. Clearly, the relevance of self-referential paradoxes can hardly be overestimated.

It is also curious to notice that Gödel used strict mathematical logic to derive his result. Analogously to the case of the local-realist assumptions of Einstein, it was the diligent and consequent application of strict mathematical logic that defeated itself *from within*. The highly abstract world of mathematics – not only physical reality – seems also to resist conformance to any literal and complete characterization. Here again, those built-in mechanisms of growth and renewal we spoke of earlier seem to ensure that we can never reach final closure. Aiming for closure is a (very human) misunderstanding of the game we are all unwittingly playing.

The principle of bivalence – the idea that everything must be true or false, this or that – is so pervasive and intrinsic to our way of 'thinking logically' that we even 'prove' things by disproving their contraries. The idea that contradiction implies fallacy, or unreality, is so deeply ingrained in our mind that we often argue that something must be true because, were it not to be so, a contradiction would arise. All this is based on the principle of bivalence, which might just as well be called the 'principle of literal truth alone.' Yet, as we have seen, bivalence is fundamentally grounded in a realist *assumption*: on the idea – the correspondence theory of truth – that the truth or falsity of every statement about the world depends on the existence or non-existence of corresponding strongly-objective facts in the world.

Therefore, *if scientific evidence ultimately forces us to reject realism, we may have to reject the principle of bivalence along with it*. If realism were to fail, the correspondence theory of truth would become void and there would be no substantiation for bivalence. Contradiction, paradox, and absurdity would have to be recognized as valid aspects of the world; indeed, as valid as the well-organized, causally-closed, linear world of our ego-consciousness. How could this be? What cosmology or worldview could make sense of it? How could we organize our thoughts or extract conclusions about our condition as living beings under circumstances like these? There are very reasonable answers to these questions. Absurdity does not need to imply a complete lack of bearings for navigating the world. From the next chapter on, we will begin to outline a hypothetical scenario that may, if you will, 'make sense of the absurd' – contradiction intended.

I want to close this chapter with a brilliant passage by Pulitzer prize-winning author Douglas Hofstadter, where he discusses the work of Dutch graphic artist M. C. Escher, particularly Escher's 1940 woodcut titled *Metamorphosis II*.[19] This and many others of Escher's works are depictions of self-referential, closed loops of images loaded with double-meanings. The images defy literal interpretation, for whenever you think you have discovered what they represent, another interpretation ambushes you. The loops typically consist of different levels of images, each level seamlessly merging into the next level through its double-meaning, until the whole thing returns to where it began. Hofstadter wrote:

> One level in a drawing might clearly be recognizable as
> representing fantasy or imagination; another level would be
> recognizable as reality. ... For any one level, there is always
> another level above it of greater 'reality,' and likewise, there
> is always a level below, 'more imaginary' than it is. This can
> be mind-boggling in itself. However, what happens if the
> chain of levels is not linear, but forms a loop? What is real,
> then, and what is fantasy?[20]

Chapter 5

Constructing reason

As we have seen, much of our logic is grounded in the so-called 'principle of bivalence' – the idea that any statement about the world has a *determinate truth-value*: it is either true or false, regardless of our ability to find out which. It is this principle that made us look upon the semantic paradoxes of the previous chapter as paradoxical at all. If we abandoned bivalence, it would not be a problem that certain things could be both true and false; such possibility would be just natural and perfectly reasonable. Indeed, bivalence underlies our standard notion that the world must be literal: by entailing that each alternative excludes its opposite, it is bivalence that implicitly drives us to believe that, if two explanations are contradictory, then if one is true the other must be false. This is the very definition of literalism. If we abandoned bivalence, we would have to abandon the notion of literal truth along with it: if an explanation could be true *and* false, then its aspect of falsity would open the door for other contradictory explanations to be true as well. As such, the world would be more like the unfolding of cognitive metaphors than a system of fixed truths; more like an evocative dream than a causally-closed mechanism.

As we have also seen, it is the assumption of realism that grounds bivalence through the correspondence theory of truth: every statement must correspond to a strongly-objective fact of the external world that determines its truth-value – that is, which determines whether the statement is true or false. If the experimental confirmation of quantum mechanics' predictions about entanglement forces us to abandon realism, then we will lose the correspondence theory of truth and will be left with no grounds to hold on to the principle of bivalence. As philosopher

Sir Michael Dummett put it, 'If the statements ... do not relate to such an external reality, the supposition that each of them possesses such a determinate truth-value is empty. ... We have, in such case, ... to take them as having been given meaning in a different way, namely by associating them with conditions of a different kind.'[1] These 'conditions of a different kind,' alluded to by Dummett, lie at the heart of the scenario we are slowly unpacking in this book. But let us not get ahead of ourselves.

Would abandoning bivalence imply abandoning logic? Without some form of logic we could no longer communicate meaningfully. It is logic that provides us with a basis for reflection and philosophical discourse.[2] Could there be another 'version' of logic that did not incorporate the principle of bivalence, but which still provided us with a coherent framework for reasoning about the world? Indeed, what I have been referring to as 'logic' is simply our standard, classical articulation of logic, which is grounded in a number of so-called 'axioms': assumed truths about reality that are deemed not to require justification. The axioms of classical logic include the principle of bivalence. By choosing different axioms, we can basically construct a new logic.

And as luck would have it, we do not need to do that from scratch. Philosophers have already developed – motivated by dilemmas different from the ones that brought us here – a logic where the principle of bivalence is abandoned. Such logic is called 'intuitionism.'[3] Sir Michael Dummett, quoted above, has been one of the key modern philosophers behind intuitionism.

Here is how it works: to the intuitionist, it is not enough to show that something cannot be false in order to claim that it must be true. Since intuitionism rejects bivalence, the fact that something is conclusively not false does *not* necessarily mean that it is true. The intuitionist must *separately* demonstrate the truth of any statement by showing how it is that it is true; that is, he or she must develop an intuition about why it is true. I know this is hard to assimilate, but bear with me; it gets easier.

Intuitionistic logic was created by mathematicians to solve mathematical problems. Its development was a reaction to mathematical realism: the idea that mathematical objects are objective, lying in wait in the kind of 'platonic world' suggested by Penrose,[4] independent of our ability to find or understand them. As such, humans do not invent mathematics but *discover* it. Mathematical realism is analogous to the broader realism we have been discussing thus far, just ported onto the abstract world of mathematics. According to it, the truth of mathematical statements is conditional on the strongly-objective existence of the corresponding mathematical objects in that hypothetical platonic realm.

This was fine and well until around the turn of the 20th century, when new problems in set theory posed new challenges for mathematical realism. A group of mathematicians and logicians, led by Dutch mathematician Luitzen Brouwer, could not fathom the strongly-objective reality of some uncountable infinities emerging from set theory. They were the first intuitionists. Their conundrum was much akin to the one facing us now, but restricted to the world of mathematics: having rejected mathematical realism, they were also left without a correspondence theory of truth for mathematical statements. If there were no strongly-objective mathematical objects, on the basis of what could one decide if a mathematical statement was true or false? They needed 'conditions of a different kind,' as Dummett said, to decide the truth-value of mathematical statements. The solution they came up with bears enormous relevance to our present discussion.

The idea is as simple as it is inescapable: if we do not have a strongly-objective mathematical world to ground the truth of our statements, then we have no alternative but to ground it in *our mind*. Think about it: there is no other possibility. So the challenge transposes into a quest for a coherent articulation of truth conditions that are grounded in mental processes, as opposed to an external world.

What the intuitionists proposed was that *mathematical objects are meaningful only insofar as they can be mentally constructed*. As such, intuitionists only accept the truth of a mathematical object if they can find a coherent mental *procedure* for generating the object. In other words, for them, truth is the outcome of a cognitive 'operation' in mind. The truth and meaning of a mathematical object are inherently associated with the existence of a 'cognitive story' that produces the object at its conclusion. If one cannot devise such a story, then the object has no meaning or truth whatsoever: it is not merely undiscovered, it is *non-existent*.

Intuitionism entails a *constructivist* worldview in mathematics: a view according to which the truth, meaning, and very existence of a mathematical object hold only insofar as the object can be *constructed* in mind by the operation of some coherent cognitive procedure. For instance, in order to show that it is true that numbers with certain properties or solutions to certain equations exist, the intuitionist must be able to generate *examples* of such numbers and solutions through a mathematical derivation procedure.

Now notice how such constructivism leads naturally to the abandonment of bivalence: even if the falsity of a mathematical statement can be ruled out, intuitionists cannot conclude that the statement is true unless and until they have a cognitive construction for the mathematical objects the statement refers to. In the example of the previous paragraph, it is not enough to merely show that the numbers or solutions cannot *not* exist; examples of the numbers and solutions must be constructible through a cognitive procedure. Before this is accomplished, the statement refers to non-existing entities and its truth, therefore, cannot be asserted. To the intuitionist, mathematical objects only come into existence after they have been coherently built in mind. This way, refutation of falsity does *not* imply truth. Bivalence does not hold.

Let me try to say the same thing again in another way, in case this is getting hard to digest. An argument of the form 'There is no way this theorem could be false, therefore it can only be true' is utterly hollow and meaningless to the intuitionist. The argument assumes that the truth of the theorem is independently determined by facts in a platonic world 'out there,' even though we do not have access to those facts. But intuitionism denies this: we can only speak of facts insofar as we can construct these facts cognitively. That we could not argue for the falsity of the theorem says nothing of our ability to construct the fact of its truth. *If the facts are cognitive creations, the principle of bivalence makes no sense.* Moreover, this constructivist view renders the lack of bivalence completely unproblematic: it is a worldview wherein non-bivalence makes *good sense*. Clearly, constructivism and the abandonment of bivalence go hand in hand.

Now notice that, so far, we have been talking about intuitionism only in the context of abstract mathematical objects. We have to be careful if we want to extrapolate the thinking behind intuitionism to the broader discussion about whether realism or idealism holds sway in the world at large; in other words, if we want to talk about tables, chairs, and people, not just abstract mathematical objects. But, as it turns out, Dummett successfully argued that the historical debate about whether the world is independent of mind is analogous to the debate between mathematical realism and intuitionism.[5] Indeed, the development of the logic and philosophy of intuitionism mirrors the problem we have been facing in this book. While we are confronted with the failures of realism in general, of the correspondence theory of truth, and of the principle of bivalence in the world of tables, chairs, and people, the intuitionists were confronted with the failures of mathematical realism, of the correspondence theory of truth, and of the principle of bivalence in the world of abstract mathematical objects. It is therefore legitimate for us to leverage the decades of reflection and articulation that went into the development of intuitionism in our own discussion. The obvious move is to extrapolate the constructivist worldview of intuitionism, along with the non-bivalent logic underpinning it, to the world of tables, chairs, and people. In doing so, I must take sole responsibility for the speculations that we will engage in from now on, as they are not implied by intuitionism.

If we extrapolate intuitionism towards the world at large, we may say that abandoning realism in general implies *a worldview according to which objects exist only insofar as they are constructed through the operation of a cognitive procedure;* that is, only insofar as they are explicitly imagined into existence. The world, according to this view, is fundamentally a conception of mind. What we experience around ourselves is what I shall call a consensus 'world-instantiation': a *particular manifestation* of the underlying, formless mental potentials intrinsic to reality, constructed according to stories we tell ourselves about what is allowed to be true or factual. We seem to filter out, before it even comes to light, everything we tell ourselves does not fit the bill: discontinuities of the main storyline, inconsistencies, and absurdity. Since we seem to construct this story together, our consensus world-instantiation is weakly-objective. Bivalence only holds sway in it to the extent that we make it part of our cognitive stories – that is, to the extent that we construct truths and falsities according to well-formed dichotomous pairs – but it is not inherent to it. Moreover, since we use language structures to tell ourselves all these stories, the consensus world-instantiation we create is, at bottom, prone to paradox anyway, as logicians, mathematicians, and physicists alike seem to have found out.

When we are sufficiently relaxed, distracted, stressed, perturbed, intoxicated, or in any way disconnected from our critical selves, the absurd may slip through the filters of our mental story-telling and spring before us, to our shock and amazement.

This may happen when we dream (like Jung's patient); when we are exposed to certain psychoactive substances (like the DMT study volunteer); when we meditate (as Jung himself did, using his method of 'active imagination');[6] when we sincerely invoke or expect the absurd (perhaps like the witnesses of the Miracle of the Sun at Fátima); when we are not yet fully caught up in the cultural paradigm of the time (perhaps like Joe Simonton); or when we trick our own filters by disguising the absurd under the cloak of something mysterious but with the potential to fit into the main storyline (perhaps like the Hessdalen lights or the Hudson valley sightings).

It is easy to see now why the volunteers of the clinical study on DMT insisted so vehemently that their experiences were real; why many 'alien abductees' are relentless in arguing for the reality of their experiences; why Joe Simonton spoke so matter-of-factly about the origin of his pancakes; why Jung insisted on the reality of the psyche: in the exact same way as our consensus world-instantiation, their *imagined* experiences were real.

But this raises another issue. When the absurd springs into the consciousness of certain individuals, there may be a split between our consensus world-instantiation and the 'smaller scale' world-instantiations that these individuals temporarily (co-)construct and experience. Many 'alien abductees' are never reported to have gone missing during the time they were supposedly abducted. The doctors and nurses watching over the DMT study volunteers did not see roadside elves. We could, therefore, hypothesize that, under certain circumstances, our consciousness can 'unplug' – 'de-tune' if you will – from the story playing in the consensus world-instantiation and tune into a more or less private world-instantiation with a different storyline; yet no less real because of it. In other cases, like the Miracle of the Sun, so many people are involved that one may think either of a group split into an alternative but still consensus world-instantiation, or of a local fluctuation in the storyline of our ordinary consensus world-instantiation. The latter would differ from a split in that it would have been witnessed by anyone within the range of the fluctuation. Finally, our idealist speculations may also open the door to the possibility of other co-existing, collective, 'large scale' consensus world-instantiations partaken of by other unknown groups of conscious entities, playing out in parallel with our own. One may even speculate whether tuning into those other 'large scale' consensus storylines would be possible for us.

The adoption of a non-bivalent, seemingly paradoxical logic as the basis of what we might call 'the new rational' comes hand in hand with the realization that the world we experience is a cognitive construct of mind. These are the two sides of the same coin: an idealist world, as it turns out, is a world of potential paradox and contradiction; *a world amenable to the absurd*. It is, in fact, a world of 'strange loops,' perpetually cycling through self-negating metaphors of themselves, like an Escher drawing, from fantasy to seeming literalism and ultimately back to fantasy.

Yet it would be unfortunate to misconstrue this picture as justifying 'relativism,' the position that any view or opinion is just as good as any other, for the world is whatever we make of it anyway; that everybody is right, regardless of how preposterous or foolish their positions or arguments might be. *No, this is not what I am saying here.* While we cannot judge statements anyone might make about private experiences, or experiences originating from any other supposed split from the main storyline of our consensus world-instantiation, those statements are only meaningful within these split-off storylines and bear no relevance to the consensus world-instantiation we normally share. And when one claims that one's statements are valid within our shared, consensus world-instantiation, *there certainly are criteria – rules of evidence – to decide on the validity of such statements.* Let us look into this in more detail.

As I articulated in my earlier book, *Dreamed up Reality*, even if individuals had absolute freedom to create their own world-instantiation, whenever they did it *together*, collaboratively, a common set of constraints would naturally and unavoidably emerge, which all participants would become subjected to. It is this emerging, shared set of constraints that provides criteria for judging the truth or falsity of statements made within the context of our shared world-instantiation. Think of the collective dream we talked about earlier, where no individual dreamer could change the dream on a whim, since the dream was an amalgamation of many inputs. Moreover, like the mass of an enormous crowd moving in unison, a collaborative world-instantiation on this scale would acquire unfathomable momentum and become seemingly autonomous; as if it had a will of its own, independent of the will of each person in the crowd.

Another metaphor to help visualize how a collaboratively constructed world-instantiation may be independent of individual will is the uncanny global behavior of ant colonies: although there is supposedly nothing more to a colony than individual ant minds, a seemingly integrated and autonomous global behavior emerges out of the interactions between individual ants, like a kind of virtual 'ant overmind.' As Prof. Andries Engelbrecht put it, 'These complex behaviors emerge from the collective behavior of very unsophisticated individuals.'[7] Each ant is largely powerless to change the momentum of the collective behavior: an ant cannot alter the 'laws of the overmind' just as we cannot alter the laws of nature. As a matter of fact, this ant overmind is so smart that scientists in the field of artificial intelligence try to emulate its strategies to solve very difficult engineering problems[8] (so much for the limitations of ant brains). The global behavior of ant colonies is an example of what, in science and philosophy, is called 'emergence.'[9] Here, I am postulating that our consensus world-instantiation is, in part, an emergent idealist phenomenon.

Because of its emergent pseudo-autonomy and the momentum behind it, it is perfectly legitimate to articulate rules of evidence that hold sway within our consensus world-instantiation: rules that determine what conditions must be fulfilled for a statement to be declared true. It is also perfectly conceivable that a participant – and thereby co-creator – of our consensus world-instantiation could make utterances about it that, according to these criteria, would be fallacies. This is the first reason why our idealist picture leaves very limited room for relativism. But there is yet another reason.

As discussed, intuitionism holds that the reality of all mathematical facts is grounded in our ability to construct these facts according to a *coherent* mental procedure; that is, a mental procedure that is internally consistent and organized as a unified whole. When we extrapolate intuitionism to a general worldview beyond mathematics alone – as we are now doing – we must give this some thought. After all, from an idealist perspective, the requirement of coherence may seem arbitrary: why would mind *have* to construct our consensus world-instantiation coherently, according to internally consistent procedures? Would free-running chaos not be a more natural and less constrained thing to expect? Yet the laws of nature we experience seem extraordinarily self-consistent, as any physicist could tell you. Therefore, if for no other reason, we may be forced to import that aspect of intuitionism into our worldview on empirical grounds: despite entropy, nature exhibits remarkably coherent patterns, so the cognitive procedure that constructs our consensus world-instantiation must indeed operate coherently and self-consistently.

It is uncomfortable to adopt a restrictive idea without some tentative conception of why it should be necessary. So I will risk one: if we observe human behavior, we find an innate, incredibly powerful need to find *closure*. We feel compelled to try and understand why things happen the way they do, as well as to anticipate what will happen next so we are not caught off guard. In order for us to find closure in this way, nature *must* operate according to organized, stable, internally consistent, and ultimately understandable patterns and regularities. After all, in chaos no reasons make sense and no predictions work; no closure can be found in chaos. To the extent that our human drives are reflections of primary, archetypal dispositions of mind, this could be the reason why our consensus world-instantiation is as coherent and internally consistent as it seems to be: mind may create it this way in an ongoing attempt to find closure about itself.

There is more to be said about this dichotomy between chaos and order. After all, an idealist worldview, wherein even principles of logic are not fundamental but constructed, opens up so much room for chaos that it becomes impossible to explain away its apparent absence.[10] *There must be chaos lying somewhere, even if it is not immediately discernible.* And there is. As a matter of fact, there may be more of it than we could comprehend or bear, hiding in the last place where we would look for it, ready to ambush us all. But this is a topic for a later chapter. For now, let us return to the question we were addressing: Why does the idealist worldview we are developing *not* entail the anything-goes of relativism? What criteria do we have for grounding truth and falsity within a world-instantiation? We have discussed one answer: that the emerging constraints of a collectively constructed world-instantiation provide us with such conditions. Now we are in the process of developing the second, complementary answer.

And here it is: since our consensus world-instantiation is constructed *coherently*, as we inferred above, then it is necessarily an interconnected and internally consistent whole. As such, it provides us with boundary conditions for determining the validity of statements: *statements are not true if they are not consistent with other aspects of the world-instantiation.* This is a coherentist view of truth: the validity of a statement depends solely on whether it coheres within a context, not on strongly-objective facts lying somewhere 'out there.' Let us review a simple example from arithmetic to gain some intuition about what this means in practice.

We learned in school that multiplying two negative numbers results in a positive number. If you remember, this was always a bit of a puzzle. We could understand, for instance, why (+2) x (-1) = (-2), since doubling a debt only increases the debt and so it is natural that the result should be negative. But (-2) x (-1) = (+2) was a whole different story. How can we get out of debt by multiplying a debt by another debt? What could possibly make this true? Assume that we are not mathematical realists. In other words, assume that there is no 'platonic world' outside our mind where (-2) x (-1) = (+2) is an independent, strongly-objective fact. So we are free to *construct* the truth of this multiplication as we fancy. We could, in principle, define it to be anything we liked. But unless we are willing to abandon mathematical meaning, we should like to define it so it remains *consistent* with the rest of the *coherent* system of arithmetic. Indeed, if we require arithmetic to remain the same for negative numbers, we can write:

$$(+2) \times (-1) + (-2) \times (-1) = (2 - 2) \times (-1) = 0 \times (-1) = 0$$

Arithmetic also allows us to perform these operations in a different order, without changing the end result. So, starting from the beginning again, we can make:

$$(+2) \times (-1) + (-2) \times (-1) = (-2) + (-2) \times (-1) = 0$$

Therefore, it must be the case that (-2) x (-1) = (+2), otherwise the end result would not continue to be zero.[11]

Conclusion: from a coherentist perspective, it is true that the multiplication of two negative numbers results in a positive number, since this is the only alternative that is consistent with the rest of arithmetic. The truth condition here has nothing to do with a strongly-objective 'realm' somewhere, but is entirely constructed by mind. All we did was to require consistency with our own, coherent, mind-created arithmetic world-instantiation. That alone provided us with solid conditions for asserting a basic truth. If someone came tomorrow and said '(-2) x (-1) = (-2) because I make it so!' such statement would be recognizably foolish even to a young student; there is clearly little room for relativism here. Now imagine this exact same argument applied not to the abstract world-instantiation of arithmetic, but to the empirical, consensus world-instantiation of tables and chairs; you will then immediately grasp what was meant with the second answer above (which you might want to quickly read again).

Note that the argumentation of the second answer holds even for a world-instantiation constructed by a single mind; it does not depend, like our first answer, on constraints emerging out of a collective construction. Hence, either way, *we always have rules of evidence* implied by the manner in which a world-instantiation has been put together. Relativism does not hold sway within any given world-instantiation, only *across* world-instantiations.

My insistence on the limitations of relativism in our consensus world-instantiation may seem to contradict my earlier assertions that open-mindedness and theoretical creativity in physics are good things. Indeed, it seems to contradict my open enthusiasm for the creation of ontological myths in general. After all, if the truths of the world are already set by (emergent) coherence constraints outside our individual control, what is the use of creating new myths? Well, here is the thing: we do not have a causally-closed, complete myth today that 'explains' everything going on. In fact, we are incredibly far from it, as I sought to illustrate in Chapter 6 of my book *Rationalist Spirituality*. Therefore, the web of coherence constraints currently grounding truth in our consensus world-instantiation is filled with gaps, like a piece of fabric covered in holes. In these gaps the crowd has not yet assembled; the ant queen has formed no colony; no momentum has yet built. There, we are only partially tied up by consistency requirements; the boundary conditions are sparse and weak; there is still freedom to create new myths. As Harpur pointed out, some subatomic particles whose existence was originally predicted purely in theory obligingly turned up as if imagined into existence;[12] they were new myths that covered gaps in the fabric of our worldview without implying (too many) contradictions elsewhere. Over time, these new myths – at least the ones that eventually become popular and gather momentum – slowly propagate through the web of coherence relationships and infect the entire story, altering our consensus views of what is true or plausible. This, it seems to me, is the way to enrich the world.

Indeed, as suggested above, the existence of clear criteria for judging truth in our consensus world-instantiation at any given moment in time does not necessarily mean that its truths are unchanging and eternal. An idealist world is one where construction is an ongoing process driven by cognitive story-telling or myth-making. If we begin to change the stories we tell ourselves, the consensus will eventually shift and we will inevitably be confronted with a changing world-instantiation. Indeed, even if the construction procedure is fairly robust and stable, it is hard to conceive that it would not drift over time: a crowd moving in unison may move very slowly, *but it does move.* If so, what people could have construed to be very reasonable and demonstrable facts, say, five or six hundred years ago (let alone thousands), would not be quite the same as what we construe to be demonstrably true today. This kind of speculation immediately brings to mind scholars of the Renaissance period, for instance, who believed very matter-of-factly in things we might today consider 'magical.'[13] Although none of us were there to see what was happening then, we – somewhat simplistically and carelessly, I might say – decree those scholars to have been merely ignorant and superstitious.

Indeed, it should be interesting to look not only at the evolution of general beliefs in our culture over time, but also at the different worldviews science itself has held during the course of its history. Since science bases its views on hard empirical observations and careful experimentation, this should give us a more substantial perspective on how the construction procedure behind our consensus world-instantiation might have evolved over time. The observations made by Thomas Kuhn on the historical evolution of scientific theories are very interesting in this regard.[14] Kuhn is likely the most influential philosopher of science since the mid-20th century, a highly respected scholar who no serious thinker ignores today. To be sure, Kuhn stops just short of taking a clear metaphysical position in his work: he simply makes historical observations based on the documentation available. Having said that, the observations he makes are quite consistent with our speculations here.

A usual view of science early in the 20th century – and still prevailing to this day among most people – was the positivist idea that science embodies a steady accumulation and refinement of objective knowledge about the world; that science never 'backtracks.' According to this view, scientific knowledge progresses monotonically over time, drawing ever closer to the ultimate truths of nature. The scientific models of yesteryears were farther from the truth than those of today, which in turn are farther from the truth than those of tomorrow. At every step in the steady progress of scientific understanding, impartial data collected from experiments serve as neutral criteria for objectively and conclusively choosing among competing scientific theories. These criteria enable a *progressive refinement* of scientific theories over time. Or so the story goes.

Kuhn thrashed this view of science by means of a thorough

historical analysis of how science has *actually* evolved over the centuries. Central to his views is the notion of a *paradigm:* a set of basic assumptions, values, and beliefs held by scientists about how the world is put together. He showed that objective data cannot be gathered and interpreted outside the context of a paradigm: the data are not neutral. It is the underlying paradigm that enables scientists to choose, among the myriad things that can be measured about the world, which ones are relevant. It is also the paradigm that enables the collected data – the 'mere facts' – to be at all interpretable; without it, the data would be, in the words of William James, just a 'blooming, buzzing confusion.'[15] Either way, *the body of beliefs embedded in the paradigm is already implicit in the collection and interpretation of the 'mere facts.'*[16] Finally, *it is also the paradigm that determines which explanations for the observed 'facts' are acceptable or to be preferred.* Indeed, we know that the inductive validity of any (scientific) conclusion is based solely on the idea that the conclusion is more probable than not.[17] For instance, we cannot know for certain that the laws of physics are the same throughout space and across time, but it seems more probable than not, so science bases the entire edifice of its cosmology on this inductive conclusion. It is the paradigm of the time that motivates scientists to determine which inferences are more probable and, therefore, which inductive conclusions are valid. In other words, it is the paradigm that provides criteria for stating whether a hypothesis is scientifically legitimate or mere metaphysical mumbo-jumbo. Since science is fundamentally grounded in inductive reasoning, the paradigm largely defines what science considers to be true or plausible at any point in its history. And now the crucial point Kuhn makes: *paradigms change over time, and along with them that which science considers to be true or reasonable.* Moreover, there is no historical evidence to suggest that these changes are a result of a continuous refinement of standards. In fact, they seem arbitrary.

Here is an example of the above: Prior to Newton, the

standards, values, and beliefs – the reigning paradigm – of science were such that any legitimate explanation for natural phenomena should be based exclusively on the shape, size, position, and movement of small corpuscles of matter acting on each other through *contact*; in other words, thoroughgoing materialism. When Newton postulated that gravity was a fundamental force innately acting between *distant* bodies, irreducible to contact between corpuscles, his proposal was ridiculed by many at the time. Gravity, as defined by Newton, was looked upon as an 'occult quality;' an appeal to 'magical' and nonsensical metaphysics; mumbo jumbo, if you like. As we now know, Newton's view eventually won out and gravity – though still a kind of 'magical' interaction at a distance – was for centuries accepted as a reasonable, scientifically legitimate, fundamental property of matter. What was once mumbo jumbo had become enshrined on the altar of science as the highest expression of scientific enlightenment. Newton had become a veritable seer of the truth.

But it was not to last: Einstein eventually came into the picture and argued that there is no such 'magical force.' Gravitational 'attraction' is simply a distortion of the fabric of space-time caused by the presence of matter. So today we are back again to the standards of thoroughgoing materialism that preceded Newton, with the difference that we must now accept space-time itself to be a 'thing' that can be bent and twisted – a bit of a magical idea in itself, one might say. This example illustrates that not only do scientific standards about what constitutes a legitimate hypothesis change, they also change non-monotonically. In other words, the standards are not being raised and getting ever closer to an ideal, but go back and forth over time. Changes of standards can be reversed and, each time, we are led to believe that we now, finally, have figured out the right standards. The history of science, as highlighted by Kuhn, shows us how naïve this belief is.

Kuhn showed that science evolves according to two recurring and intercalated phases, which he termed 'normal science' and 'scientific revolutions.' In the phase of 'normal science,' scientific development proceeds by refinement of the reigning paradigm. No attempt is made to test or challenge it, but every attempt is made to reinforce its foundations. Indeed, Kuhn highlights the role of paradigm-driven *expectation* in the process of data collection and interpretation during this phase, and how it seems to turn the paradigm into a kind of self-fulfilling prophecy. It is only when enough anomalies – which, I might add, show up when scientists begin to look at those holes in the fabric of the consensus world-instantiation wherein not enough momentum has yet gathered – accumulate over time that scientists are forced to begin rethinking the paradigm. Science development then enters the phase of a 'scientific revolution:' the most fundamental assumptions about how the world works are then up for grabs. The outcome of a 'scientific revolution' is the creation of a new paradigm: a new worldview entailing a new set of assumptions, beliefs, and values; new guidelines for what constitutes acceptable inductive reasoning. Thereafter, scientific development again enters a phase of 'normal science' and the cycle repeats itself. Kuhn has shown that, surprisingly, subsequent paradigms are often *incompatible* with earlier ones: what before was absurd and inconceivable suddenly becomes the embodiment of reason; and vice-versa. Science does not progress through a steady refinement of a worldview, but by throwing out worldviews in favor of new, previously unthinkable ones. One cannot help but wonder which of the certainties we currently hold about the world will have to be discarded in the near future. Finally, Kuhn also points out that there is no historical basis for believing that scientific theories of the past, which we now consider out of date and plain wrong, were any less scientific than today's theories. As a matter of fact, these past theories seem to have explained the empirical observations of their time just as well as our current theories explain the empirical observations of today. As Kuhn marvelously put it, 'If these out-of-date beliefs are to be called *myths*, then *myths* can be produced by the same sorts of methods and held for the same sorts of reasons that now lead to scientific knowledge'[18] (emphasis added).

Central to Kuhn's description of the scientific development process is the 'paradigm-ladenness' of data, which I alluded to above. What this means is that there is no such thing as impartial, unbiased, purely objective data. All collection and interpretation of data is laden with the assumptions and beliefs behind the reigning paradigm. As Kuhn put it, referring to a number of psychological experiments in which the subjects' expectations largely determined what they perceived, 'surveying the rich experimental literature ... makes one suspect that something like a paradigm is prerequisite to perception itself. What a man sees depends upon what he looks at and also upon what his previous visual-conceptual experience has taught him to see.'[19] The implication of this is that the usefulness of the idea of strongly-objective facts – if not the idea itself – is called into question.[20] After all, if the facts, as perceived, are themselves infected with the assumptions of a paradigm, the correspondence theory of truth fails. Moreover, 'strange loops' emerge in scientific debate: When the choice of the right paradigm is at issue, groups defending different paradigms interpret the data at hand – the 'facts' – according to their own choice of paradigm. Kuhn: 'When paradigms enter, as they must, into a debate about paradigm choice, their role is necessarily circular. ... This issue of paradigm choice can never be unequivocally settled by logic and experiment alone.'[21] Clearly, *self-reference* is fundamentally embedded in the development of any scientific worldview, the implications of which, in light of earlier discussions, are uncanny.

Kuhn goes as far as to suggest that the very world scientists live in – in terms of their perception gestalts – *changes* after a paradigm transition, so that scientists actually begin to *see* different things. 'When paradigms change, the world itself changes with them.'[22] Despite emphasizing in his 1969 postscript that he does not reject realism, Kuhn explains that human beings – scientists included – are limited to what they can perceive.[23] So if a change of paradigm fundamentally alters what is perceived, *it all works just as though nature itself had changed*. Now, since we have no direct access to strongly-objective facts 'out there,' but only to our perceptions of them, who is to say that this is not actually the case?

To support his views on this issue, Kuhn brings up several intriguing historical cases. He mentions, for instance, the case of Sir William Herschel's discovery of Uranus.[24] As you may know, planets can be distinguished from stars in the night sky by observation of their motion: whereas stars do not move with respect to each other, planets do move with respect to stars. As it turns out, prior to Sir William's discovery, there were over a dozen documented observations of a star in the position we now know was occupied by Uranus at the time. One of the observers had actually looked at this 'star' during four consecutive nights without noticing the obvious motion that would have given it away as a planet. Were the *expectations* of these early astronomers leading them to actually see a fixed star where we now see a planet? Were these merely equivocated perceptions or the reflection of a different storyline determining what our consensus world-instantiation looked like at the time?

In another example, Kuhn mentions the earlier 'effluvium' theories of electricity. The first observations of electrical phenomena are thought to have been of amber attracting chaff particles after having been rubbed with fur. Around the turn of the 17th century, scientists postulated that an invisible elastic substance – called 'effluvium' – stretched out in space trying to hold two objects together.[25] It was this substance that supposedly pulled the chaff particles to the piece of amber or other electrified objects. Clearly, this theory could only account for electrostatic *attraction*, not *repulsion*. As Kuhn notes, it is documented that scientists occasionally saw chaff particles 'bouncing off' electrified bodies or 'falling off' them.[26] In other words, they did not see electrical repulsion, but only the usual mechanical or gravitational forces in action. Yet, to any observer today, the *repulsion* of chaff particles by an electrified body would be obvious, incontrovertible, unambiguous; nobody would ever mistake that for chaff rebounding or falling off. Is it possible that, back then, scientists simply *saw* that which they could conceive and, therefore, expected?

Kuhn goes on to offer other similar examples. His case is quite compelling. While he wisely avoids their metaphysical implications – opting instead to stick to epistemic phenomenalism *à la* Immanuel Kant's 'transcendental aesthetics'[27] – his observations match quite naturally, and most economically, with the idealist, constructivist worldview we have been elaborating on. Therefore, it seems that wherever we look – quantum physics, major world events, the foundations of logic, analytic philosophy, and now the history of science – we see the subtle footprints of a dreamed-up reality; a reality where logic is itself constructed through a self-imposed reduction in the degrees of freedom of the absurd; a world constructed through coherent mental procedures; a world where empirical observation is a mirror of the subjects' implicit worldview.

To close this chapter, I would like to mention one more of Kuhn's observations; one that is particularly telling in the context of our considerations. In Kuhn's own words: 'Once it has achieved the status of paradigm, a scientific theory is declared invalid only if an alternate candidate is available to take its place. No process yet disclosed by the historical study of scientific development at all resembles the methodological stereotype of falsification by direct comparison with nature.'[28] *It seems that we must always have a story – a myth – or the world itself would vanish before our eyes.*

Chapter 6

The reality within

In previous chapters, we have seen that the subjective world of mind may be closer to the objective world of matter than most of us ever dared suspect. In fact, these two worlds may be one and the same. Therefore, a more thorough understanding of mind and its most familiar manifestation, the human psyche, becomes paramount and urgent. Not only is it relevant for our grasp of our own feelings and motivations, but now also for making sense of the world at large. If the dichotomy between subjectivity and objectivity breaks down, psychology becomes the wellspring of physics.

The human psyche is far from being restricted to our ordinary feelings and perceptions. Indeed, most of the psyche is buried deep beneath the threshold of metacognitive introspection. Much of what governs our emotions, motivations, reactions, and even our views, lies hidden in areas of the psyche that we have come to call the 'unconscious.' As I mentioned earlier, the term 'unconscious' is unfortunate, for mental contents inaccessible through metacognitive introspection do not necessarily lack phenomenal properties. In other words, we may well *experience* the contents of the 'unconscious,' but simply not know *that* we experience them. Having said this, I shall continue to use the word 'unconscious,' without further scare quotes, for the sake of readability and consistency with the literature on depth psychology.

The unconscious aspects of our personalities manifest themselves indirectly, through influencing our conscious thoughts, feelings, and behaviors. It was depth psychology, in the second half of the 19th century and the first half of the 20th century, led by figures like William James, Sigmund Freud, and

Carl Jung, that uncovered the existence and importance of the unconscious layers of the psyche. These men revealed to us the previously unsuspected depth of the human mind.

Of the different approaches to depth psychology that are practiced today, the Jungian approach – also called 'analytical psychology' – is, in my view, the richest. Unlike Freud, who tried to boil every human impulse down to some repressed sexual drive, Jung saw the psyche as a much more complex system. My own experiences exploring the unconscious layers of my psyche, as discussed in my earlier work, *Dreamed up Reality*, have convinced me of the accuracy of Jung's approach. To me, Jung was a true pioneer. He saw far beyond anyone else in his time, and still farther than most today. His legacy is perhaps even more important to our culture today than it was during his lifetime.

Through empirical observations of his own mental processes, and those of his countless patients, Jung drafted a kind of map of the human mind. Roughly speaking, this map divides the psyche into three main segments. The first corresponds to our regular awareness: the feelings, thoughts, perceptions, etc. that we can access through introspection; that is, those we know *that* we experience. If you ask someone to describe him- or herself and the world he or she lives in, it is mostly from the perspective of this segment that the person will speak. Because it embodies the point of view of the ego – that which defines us as individual agents operating in the context of a wider world seemingly separate from ourselves – we shall call this first segment 'ego-consciousness.' Indeed, our ability to introspect is ordinarily restricted to ego-consciousness alone. Therefore, we tend to associate our sense of identity with the perspective of the ego, ignoring the other two – much larger – segments of the psyche. In other words, we erroneously think we are our egos. Only through non-ordinary states of consciousness, like certain types of dreams and meditative states, can we gain some metacognitive awareness of the other two segments.

The second, deeper segment of the psyche is what Jung called the 'personal unconscious.' There lie aspects of our personalities – memories, thoughts, feelings, emotions, drives, etc. – which were once in ego-consciousness, but have since been forgotten, rejected, or repressed. In the course of our lives, each one of us has been different 'people:' we have held different worldviews, memories of different experiences, and expressed different behavioral patterns. Over time, much of this falls off along the way and is forgotten. But it all survives hidden in the personal unconscious. Moreover, this survival is not static: unconscious mental processes continue to operate and evolve in the personal unconscious, living a rich parallel life that we ordinarily cannot access through introspection.

Jung considered the personal unconscious to be merely the superficial layer of the unconscious mind, the part closest to ego-consciousness. The bulk of the unconscious consists of what he called the 'collective unconscious,' the third segment of the psyche. Unlike the personal unconscious, which is restricted to the mental history and idiosyncratic dreams and visions of an individual, the collective unconscious is an area of mental activity shared by all humanity – perhaps even by all conscious beings. At its level, our psyches unite and are no longer distinct. The collective unconscious is also unfathomably vast, much of it lying way deeper than ego-consciousness. Although the remote mental contents that populate it are as much a part of you as any thought, memory, or feeling you may be able to access right now, they remain beyond the reach of your ego.

The collective unconscious is partly an 'archive' of transpersonal experiences. But it is also creative and dynamic, embodying structured potentials for experience organized according to what Jung called 'archetypes': primordial templates of mental activity. And here we need to take a deep breath, because a correct understanding of the archetypes is not easy to achieve. The difficulty lies in the important distinction between what the archetypes *are* and how they *manifest* themselves. Many people take the latter for the former, which is an error. Indeed, the archetypes, in and by themselves, are ineffable: they are beyond the reach of logical, rational articulation. As Jung insisted on, an archetype in itself is 'empty.' The best we can say is that it is a template to be filled in, like the predetermined structure of a crystal before the crystal itself forms. As such, despite being in themselves 'empty,' the archetypes determine the general structure of experiences and behaviours.[1] We each 'dress' the archetypes in the clothing – that is, the symbols – that are most evocative to us. Only then can we become metacognitively aware of the archetypes' manifestations.

Some examples may be helpful at this stage. The archetype of the 'Hero' is perhaps the basic scaffolding of our modern mental lives in the West: the hero is achievement-oriented; he fights and conquers by defeating and killing his many enemies; but he also saves the innocent. The Hero embodies the notions of 'success' and 'victory,' for good or for bad. The archetype itself is just an 'empty' template: different people live out the same Hero archetype throughout the course of very different lives. Yet we can always recognize the same 'heroic' template behind their different life stories.

Similarly, the archetype of the 'Mother' – the caring, protective, nurturing entity; but also the dangerous seductress and witch – is an important template unconsciously informing our mental lives.[2] Yet another interesting example is the archetype of the 'Trickster,'[3] which bears particular relevance to our discussion in view of the inherent elusiveness and ambiguity of the calls of the absurd. Indeed, the Trickster embodies contradictoriness and defies logical bivalence. It has a highly elusive, multifold nature that manifests itself through pranks, jokes, and puns. It is morally ambiguous and deceitful, though it is also entertaining like a clown. It has a shape-shifting character difficult to pin down: whenever you think you have figured it out, it morphs into something else, just like Harpur's daimons, or an Escher drawing, or a semantic paradox. Perhaps the Trickster is the most exiled archetype in our scientistic culture. As Jung noted, since the time of the Enlightenment our 'petty reasoning minds,' which cannot endure paradoxes, have been rejecting paradoxical truths.[4] Only in special events, like carnival celebrations, do we allow a vague hint of the Trickster to briefly emerge into ego-consciousness. For the most part, we have repressed the Trickster's ambiguity and contradictoriness for the benefit of an obsessive search for explanation and closure, based on bivalence. *Yet, if there is anything about our own nature, and that of the world, which transcends logic, then obviously only through logical contradiction can we be awakened to it.* Anything that transcends logic will appear illogical and absurd, like a prank or a pun, from the point of view of logic. As such, perhaps the Trickster has a fundamental role to play in the expansion of our understanding of nature. Its exile in the deepest reaches of the unconscious is unfortunate.

Myth is the natural, primordial language of the mental processes unfolding in the collective unconscious. And since myth is not restricted by classical logic and its bivalent foundations, the collective unconscious is as conducive to chaos and absurdity as it is to order and rationality. Indeed, Jung insisted that no rational thought can come close to the richness and evocative power of mythical images. As such, the collective unconscious is inherently broader and more powerful in its ability to accommodate the diverse aspects of nature – including chaos and absurdity – than the constrained logical perspective of ego-consciousness. Moreover, the mythical images unfolding in the collective unconscious tend to reflect the ego's attitude towards the aspects of the psyche that it cannot access: if we are hostile towards the unconscious, the images become threatening; if we are friendly, the images soften.[5] Clearly, thus, the collective unconscious not only comprises chaos, but also embodies – through some layers of indirection – psychic self-reference. It is a vast vessel of self-referential chaos lying hidden in the last place we would ever care to look: *within ourselves*. Facing up to this realization is something few of us are able to do without strong resistance, for the mere intimation of chaos can already be overwhelming and disconcerting.

The natural role of the archetypes is to exert a formative influence on ego-consciousness in order to compensate for the latter's imbalances.[6] In dreams or other non-ordinary states of consciousness, archetypes can manifest in our awareness dressed in particular symbolisms; filled in with idiosyncratic contents. As such, they are experienced by ego-consciousness as autonomous figures with a life of their own. A common motif for the manifestation of archetypal images is the dwarf – similar to fairies or aliens. Dwarfs symbolize the subtle, 'small' impulses from the unconscious, which are nonetheless endowed with formative intentionality.[7]

In a dream or vision, one can have conversations with archetypal entities emerging from the unconscious as if one were talking to other people. Jung has written of having conversations with one of these archetypal entities, Philemon, while walking around his garden.[8] But we must be careful in interpreting this: *It is only from the point of view of ego-consciousness that the figures from the unconscious appear autonomous and independent of us. When we identify ourselves with our egos, we have no alternative but to interpret manifestations from all other segments of the psyche as something external to us and, therefore, autonomous, strongly-objective, and outside our control.* As a matter of fact, here may lie a hint as to why the world 'out there' seems so autonomous and separate from us, at least as far as the perspective of the ego is concerned. If, instead, we were aware of our true, fully integrated personalities, we would immediately recognize archetypal manifestations as the product of our own mind at work. Indeed, we would recognize all the transpersonal experiences unfolding in the collective unconscious as our own.

The unconscious is the realm of the unformed and the chaotic. Ego-consciousness, on the other hand, lives in a well-formed and well-determined psychic landscape. It is the ego that orders and organizes the chaotic substrate of nature according to its own rules and categories. 'You create order according to what you know,' said Jung.[9] The rules and categories of the ego are embodied in our logic and rationality. In a way, the ego reduces the unlimited degrees of freedom of the chaotic unconscious – the realm of the imagination – leaving only a narrow subset available as it attempts to create order, regularity, bivalence, and closure. From the perspective of the unconscious, the rational ego may thus be felt as an impediment, a barrier to be overcome.[10]

Another key archetype for our discussion, and arguably the most important of all archetypes, is the 'Self.' Jung defined the Self as the totality of the psyche – both conscious and unconscious segments – as well as its center.[11] The Self is thus the center of the total personality, just as the ego is the center of our ordinary, metacognitive experiential landscape. Because of its all-encompassing nature, 'the Self is a union of opposites *par excellence.'*[12] *As such, it transcends bivalence and literalism.* Yet, the definition above does not actually *describe* the Self, which Jung considered ineffable, beyond rational apprehension.[13] What the Self really is remains, therefore, a mystery.

Central to Jungian psychology is the concept of 'individuation.' According to Jung, everything that lives strives for wholeness. Individuation is the natural process by means of which the different conscious and unconscious segments of the psyche are integrated and brought under the light of metacognitive awareness, so as to achieve wholeness. Through individuation, the ego is absorbed into a broader personality.[14] The archetypes, in their compensatory role, are central to the promotion of individuation. Hypothetically, a fully individuated person would identify themselves not with the ego, but with the whole of their psyche, including all unconscious aspects. In other words, *a fully individuated person would be aware of, and identify with, the true complete Self, thereby transcending the logical, bivalent, and rational proclivities of the ego.* He or she would know much of what goes on in the deepest reaches of their mind. But since the Self is ineffable and its boundaries unknown, it is impossible to describe – and perhaps even to conceive of – what the awareness of the whole Self might entail. Jungian analysts seek to facilitate the taking of meaningful steps towards individuation by their patients, for the process itself promotes psychic balance and health.

The process of individuation is the ultimate goal of psychic life. As such, just like the manifestations of archetypal templates, it is universal. But the complexity of modern human life obscures the presence of archetypal patterns subtly guiding the human psyche towards integration. One would therefore expect to find more explicit and clear manifestations of archetypes in simpler stories and myths. And indeed, Dr. Marie-Louise von Franz, one of Jung's closest pupils, identified clear archetypal themes in the world's fairy tales.[15] The study of fairy tales is crucial because of their absolute simplicity, generality, and independence of particular cultural or racial contexts. As von Franz suggested, fairy tales are like a universal psychic language of all humanity.[16] The different characters in a fairy tale often represent different (archetypal) aspects of our mind – different segments of the Self – in the struggle for individuation. The creation and telling of fairy tales brings one into greater harmony with the unconscious,[17] something our culture thoroughly misses today.

Many fairy tales are ultimately metaphors of the process of individuation.[18] They illustrate the archetypal forces in action, promoting the integration of the psyche. If our rationality and scientism deny these forces room to play out in our ego-consciousness, they may, as Jung suggested, force themselves in through synchronistic projections onto external objects and events. The struggle for individuation may thus become externalized in the world 'out there.' This possibility, frightful as it may sound, is suggestive when one considers how uncannily reminiscent of fairy tales some of the calls of the absurd are, in their simplicity and illogical symbolisms.

We are not who we ordinarily think we are. Our psyches are not restricted to the horizon of ego-consciousness. Below the threshold of metacognitive introspection, entire mental universes, ruled by chaos and irrationality – but rich in characters, stories, and meaning – are constantly playing themselves out, deep within us. Their struggles aim at the integration of the psyche. Knowingly or unknowingly to ego-consciousness, the epic of individuation unfolds within us at all times. Through out-of-control rationalism and scientism, we have maintained our gaze pointed firmly away from the struggle within. But ultimately the tide cannot be stopped. Our only option, if Jung was correct, is to manage the process in as harmonious a manner as possible. We might indeed just as well help it along, for the prize at the end of the road is generous: the achievement of balance, peace, and the becoming of who we really are. And that which we really are may be beyond our wildest fantasies.

Chapter 7

A cosmology beyond absurdity

Depth psychology shows us that our mind is much broader and richer than the limited perspective of ego-consciousness. The vastness of the psyche far exceeds the heavily filtered cognition experienced in our waking lives, under ordinary states of consciousness. Indeed, as Jung discovered, the psyche has at least two levels beyond ego-consciousness: the personal unconscious and the collective unconscious. Jung also showed that autonomous psychic complexes are constantly at work in the unconscious: we have vast inner lives of perception, thought, and emotion lying under the surface of metacognitive awareness; inner worlds populated with many seemingly autonomous characters. Buried within us, mythopoetic stories are uninterruptedly played out, rich in symbolic and metaphorical significance and unconstrained by classical logic. Our inner worlds do not comply with bivalence, which is a superficial creation of the ego.

But here is the thing: the idealist, constructivist model we have been developing implies that the structure of the world is a mirror of the structure of the psyche. *If, as depth psychology has discovered, the psyche is layered in 'realms' ranging from ego-consciousness to the collective unconscious, then so is the world.* Insofar as mythopoetic stories constantly unfold in the unconscious, they construct mythopoetic world-instantiations just as the stories of ego-consciousness construct the physical universe. There is no reason to believe that the world-instantiations of the unconscious are any less real than our consensus world-instantiation; asserting so would be arbitrary in light of the argumentation thus far. Jung himself intuited this when he talked of the 'reality of the psyche,' though he avoided direct metaphysical assertions in this regard perhaps until his late work, *Mysterium Coniunctionis*.[1] Crucially, the ultimate map of nature may be the map of the psyche as uncovered by depth psychology. As such, depth psychology may take precedence over physics in its primacy as a description of the universe.

Since our psyches comprise unconscious layers, the unavoidable implication is that *there are unconscious world-instantiations we partake of – with different degrees of awareness – concurrently and at all times*. Our ordinary waking experiences may be merely islands betraying an unfathomable underwater mountain chain of world-instantiations. As such, our ego-consciousness may be but one viewpoint in the many levels of unfolding story-telling, all of them equally real. Let us explore the implications of this in more detail.

We have seen that, since all world-instantiations are constructs of mind, the coherence constraints they entail are also mental creations: stories we tell ourselves about what fits together and what does not. At bottom, the underlying mental potentials that form the *'prima materia'* of reality are formless and *un*constrained; assuming anything else would entail an arbitrary, *ad hoc* boundary condition. As such, the logical world of ego-consciousness is a consensus creation: logic is a coherence-enforcing, tacitly agreed set of constraints, driven by our innate need to find closure. We build a world where the story is linear, self-consistent, continuous, and where truth is seemingly literal; a world where the principle of bivalence rules supreme. Classical logic is the veil of veils: a self-imposed filter on the stories; a straitjacket of thought we wear most of our waking lives and which prevents us from seeing the nature of being for what it really is. If only we could 'turn off' classical logic for a moment, we would probably be in awe of what would become instantly clear to our cognition.

But as we go deeper into the unconscious layers of the psyche, these constraints relax, for they begin to escape the attention scope of the ego. Blinded by the light of metacognitive awareness, the ego fails to notice and stop forbidden constructs from forming in the darker recesses of the mind. The straitjackets of classical logic and language loosen up as the ego progressively forfeits its grip on the story-telling. The primordial, formless mental 'substance' of reality can then take on more unconstrained, instinctive, and perhaps more natural and authentic shapes. Absurd world-instantiations emerge, where continuity is neglected and meaning is eminently symbolic. These absurd world-instantiations are the cognitive mirrors of the myths in the personal unconscious. There lie, for instance, the worlds of our personal dreams: the universes where we fly, where characters matter-of-factly morph into other characters, where violations of causality do not raise an eyebrow, and where explanations are not linear. In these private world-instantiations we have complete freedom to sculpt a universe of our own, unconstrained. They embody the realm of metaphor, where cognitive motifs imported from our consensus world-instantiation are deployed in absurd ways, so as to evoke insights that transcend logical, linear thinking.

All these metaphorical stories are laid out according to collective archetypal patterns emerging from yet deeper realms. The archetypes do not entail stories as such, but only primordial templates around which stories can be woven. They are the basic blueprints for all the layers of story-telling constructing world-instantiations above them. Seemingly literal motifs merely 'fill in' the otherwise 'empty' archetypes, resulting in absurd happenings: suns that zigzag and fall from the sky, glowing birds flying off cliffs, small grey aliens performing reproductive experiments, and dwarfs guarding the entrances of caves. Hence, the world-instantiations of the personal unconscious have a proclivity to be grounded in an individual's personal history in our consensus world-instantiation: someone with an education in mythology will probably leverage different motifs than someone educated in mathematics. We can only live the reality of an archetype when it is 'dressed' in these motifs imported from our personal history. Therefore, the resulting scenario becomes mostly personal in its cognitive manifestation, forfeiting weak-objectivity.

At the deepest reaches of the personal unconscious – at its very boundary – we find ineffable private reveries: dreams and visions that we simply cannot put into words. These constitute private world-instantiations that entirely transcend the references and categories of 3-dimensional space and linear time; alternative universes, if you will. Though still archetypal, the unfolding of the story in these alternative universes cannot be 'filled in' with familiar motifs; it cannot be described in language. There is, indeed, not much one can communicate about the world-instantiations unfolding here, which are only knowable by acquaintance. Yet, anyone who experiences an ineffable call of the absurd will swear – as Dr. Strassman's DMT study volunteers did – that they are as real as anything, and perhaps even 'more real than real.'

As we go even deeper into the reality of mind, we reach a collective realm, the basis of the entire mountain chain of being: the world-instantiations of the collective unconscious. But whereas the realm of our consensus world-instantiation is 'collective' in the sense that experiences there – taking place under the light of metacognitive awareness – can be communicated, synchronized, and thereby shared across separate egos, this realm is more fundamentally collective: here, there is no split into seemingly separate subjects. This realm comprises weakly-objective, seemingly autonomous, ineffable stories that we cannot control individually. But aside from this collective aspect, the world-instantiations of the collective unconscious are like those of the personal unconscious in that they unfold without the constraints of logic or physics. Here, we live out our collective, most indescribable and primordial 'dreams.'

It is interesting to notice that, in between the weakly-objective realm of our consensus world-instantiation and the collective realm of the unconscious, there lies a realm – the personal unconscious – of private reveries, visions, imagination, and dreams; an 'Otherworld' scripted by stories of our own, and reflecting our personal inner attitudes. Indeed, Harpur observed that the 'Otherworld' seems to mirror the view we take of it.[2] This 'Otherworld' is also the stage for the interaction between the collective unconscious and our individual memories from consensus life: the middle ground where collective archetypes emerge dressed in the clothes and references imparted by our personal history in the physical world. In this personal theater of the imagination we create our own heaven or hell; we enact our private fantasies, fears, hopes, or whatever it is that lies hidden deep within us, below the rational surface of metacognitive awareness. The calls of the absurd indicate that these reveries are not only real but may, under certain circumstances, jut into our consensus world-instantiation. After all, the worldview we are exploring entails no reason why the separation between these realms should be definite and stable. Rather, the realms may slowly morph into each other in fluidic and relatively unstable ways, depending on our attention and 'tuning frequency.' The boundaries between them may shimmer and contort; they are just a matter of story-telling, after all.

The calls of the absurd pointed the way: they showed that there are riches lying beyond the logic-constrained stories we ordinarily live out; they suggested that depth psychology, interpreted under an idealist, constructivist worldview, provides a less epiphenomenal map of nature than physics. By following this map, we found the ground of the absurd: a world-instantiation of the unconscious, unconstrained by the ego-created restrictions of bivalence, literalism, linearity, and continuity. But by having pursued this path we are now faced with an unavoidable question: What is reality when *no stories* are being told? What happens when the gramophone grinds to a halt?

Clearly, the road does not end at the absurd. It goes deeper, into that which differentiates itself first into the *ineffable* stories of the deepest unconscious realms, then into the *metaphorical* or *symbolic* stories of the absurd, and only then into the *logical* arena of our consensus world-instantiation. We shall call this primordial mental 'substance' of reality the 'Formless.' By definition, it is impossible to characterize the Formless: if we did, it would no longer be formless, but would instead take on a literal or metaphorical form. All we can do is infer that the Formless entails templates for self-differentiation into stories, and the disposition to undergo such differentiation. Indeed,

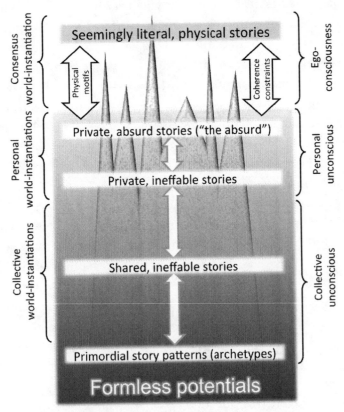

Figure 2. The cosmology of the absurd; and beyond

the blueprints for how the Formless differentiates Itself *must* be built into Itself as innate potentials, for initially there is nothing but the Formless. These blueprints are the archetypes.[3]

The speculative cosmology discussed above can be graphically summed up as in Figure 2. Let us go through it once again but, this time, from the bottom up.

In Figure 2, the Formless is represented by the invisible foundation of a submerged mountain chain: the elusive, ineffable basis for everything that protrudes from it and owes its existence to it. As the first discernible expressions of the Formless, the archetypes are represented by the unified base of the mountain chain, diffuse in the dark depths, but vaguely discernible. As we move up towards the surface, stories are subtly woven together according to these archetypal templates. At first, these stories are ineffable and completely outside the scope of space-time or language. Slowly, the mountain chain becomes better delineated and more clearly defined, until it begins differentiating itself into several discrete peaks. Though they are ultimately united by a common base, these peaks can be told apart: they represent the birth of individuality from a common matrix, in the form of our personal unconscious psyches. At this level, the shared storylines originally unfolding in the world-instantiations of the collective unconscious begin to split apart into separate world-instantiations. These are still ineffable, but as physical motifs – perceptual images originating from our consensus world-instantiation – migrate down from the realms above, they get integrated into these stories in the form of illogical metaphors. Mythopoetic reveries result: the realm of the absurd.

At the level of the personal unconscious, the differentiation of the peaks is still partial and incomplete. Their residual commonalities may allow metaphorical world-instantiations to span across peaks, acquiring some degree of weak-objectivity. What our culture cynically calls 'mass hallucinations' may perhaps arise from this. Indeed – and this is where the metaphor of Figure 2 partially breaks – this mountain chain may not be so solid: it may be malleable like magma, the distinction between peaks being fluidic and dynamic over time and space.

As we move further up, the tips of the different peaks break the surface of the ocean and emerge into daylight. They form discrete islands, apparently unconnected from the perspective of anyone looking from above the surface. Differentiation is now complete. These islands represent our individual egos: the various viewpoints from which our consensus world-instantiation is experienced. Because they are bathed in the light of metacognitive awareness, these islands can see one another. They can communicate through language – with all of language's intrinsic paradoxes – and inform each other of their private experiences. As they 'compare notes,' so to speak, synchronization naturally and automatically emerges between their cognitive landscapes. Their true universe is the absurd, metaphorical world-instantiations of their personal unconscious minds; but in their search for closure, they begin to filter out elements of those metaphorical world-instantiations that do not seem consistent with what they hear from other islands. Coherence constraints emerge, which determine what makes sense and what does not. Metaphorical motifs become seemingly literal; common sense crystallizes; bivalence is born. The crowd assembles; the ant colony is formed. Scientific paradigms are agreed upon.

The seemingly literal storyline of our consensus world-instantiation emerges out of the metaphorical worlds of the personal unconscious through the creation and enforcement of such coherence constraints. They secure the weaving of various metaphors into a linear, continuous, self-consistent, and logical story. This is an echo of the aspiration for closure intrinsic to the Formless. Indeed, no closure can be found in the chaotic worlds of the absurd. But through subtle exposure to the various inconsistent, discontinuous storylines unfolding there, filters and selection mechanisms – both embodying specific constraints – can be evolved and then applied by the ego. As we have seen when discussing why the multiplication of two negative numbers *must* result in a positive number, the process can generate, from within itself, the constraints necessary to facilitate closure. The resulting filters block out every element of the bottomless chaos that does not fit consistently into the emerging, average storyline. The selection mechanisms pick out and weave together those that do. This way, our consensus world-instantiation is simply a constrained and synchronized version of the absurd; a version squeezed into fewer degrees of freedom. But the absurd continues to simmer under the surface, in its full glory.

According to this scenario, *the aspiration for Self-understanding and closure intrinsic to the Formless is the most fundamental instinct of nature and the driving force of the entire process of differentiation* illustrated in Figure 2.

The surface of the ocean in Figure 2 represents the boundary of metacognitive awareness: everything above it is accessible through ordinary introspection; everything below is obfuscated by the light of metacognitive awareness above and can only be unveiled by an alteration of our state of consciousness. However, like in any ocean, the surface can sometimes be churned by storms: rolling waves can expose untold absurdities, allowing the islands to glimpse unexpected mysteries that have, all along, lain hidden under water. These are the calls of the absurd, reminding us that the matrix of the world lies below the surface of empirical consistency and logic.

It is tempting to wonder why individual egos cannot simply decide to tell themselves a different story, thereby changing the world they live in. It seems so simple: if different egos simply chose different coherence constraints, weak-objectivity would collapse. If this were possible, it would directly contradict observation – for we clearly cannot change our empirical world at will – and invalidate the worldview we are developing. But remember, we have covered this ground earlier: it is only the stubbornness of the local-realist mainstream view that, by assuming that individual psyches – like brains – are separate entities, motivates this fallacious objection. If you can shelve this obstinate assumption for a moment, the objection will dissolve into meaninglessness.

Indeed, when we discussed earlier the hypothetical possibility that the world is a synchronized 'dream' partaken by multiple individuals, we mentioned that individual psyches needed to be somehow interconnected for such a possibility to be conceivable. The common base of the mountain chain in Figure 2 provides the means for such interconnection. What appears to be different entities – separate mountain peaks, islands, individual egos – are actually protuberances, salient features of a single underlying matrix; mere viewpoints taken by a unified mind. The coherence constraints applied by each individual ego in the construction of our consensus world-instantiation may be shared through – perhaps even enforced by – this underlying unified matrix. The very choice of these constraints may be a choice of the matrix as a whole, simply expressed through the filters of individual egos with small, local variations and fluctuations.

Our inability to tell ourselves a different story and thereby change the world arises from the fact that we operate from the viewpoint of ego-consciousness, not of our true Self. The latter resides outside the constraints of constructed space-time. In other words, we think as characters in the play, not as actors; unlike the latter, the former are constrained by the script. But an implication of the worldview we are developing here is that our true Self should indeed be able to change the world (that It does not clearly means that It does not want to). The key issue is thus not what we can or cannot do, *but who or what we think we are*. Before we can say, in full and honest agreement with our deepest intuitions, that we can change the world, we must first find our true Self through individuation.

If bivalence is not fundamental, reality rests on an unfathomable foundation of paradoxical, metaphor-forming functions. Yet our ordered, logical, comprehensible world may, in a way, be the highest achievement of ego-consciousness: it embodies a coherent, shared creation out of the raw material of mind; a well-defined work of art carefully sculpted out of chaos. At the same time, this creation inherently imposes limits on our thoughts and worldviews. The very work of art we have every reason to be proud of is also a straitjacket that restricts us to bivalent logic and linear, causal reasoning. If we are to progress in our quest for understanding the world and our condition within it – for understanding the nature of time, space, energy, matter, life, and death – we may have to transcend the boundaries imposed by our art. We may have to shatter the hollow sculpture of our own creation, for we find ourselves imprisoned within it. We may have to acknowledge the formless foundation of chaos, of pure potential, upon which our thoughts and world rest. And then we may be able to re-sculpt the formless potentials into broader, richer, more beautiful, meaningful, and transcendent art.

Chapter 8

The Formless speaks

We are incessantly, relentlessly, tirelessly telling ourselves stories; constantly attempting to categorize and match everything we experience against some (coherent) storyline playing out in our mind. Well, at least *I* am like this, and I seem to observe others doing the same. This is why certain forms of meditation prove so challenging: there, the idea is *to stop the story-telling*. It turns out many of us require instruction, the learning of techniques developed over centuries or millennia, and years of training to have *a chance* to *momentarily* pause the story-telling; so inborn it seems to be. Some people even feel that they need to isolate themselves completely, in mountains or monasteries, for years at a time, to stop telling themselves what is or might be going on.

So it is no wonder that we are prisoners of the consensus world-instantiation we build, to the point that many of us – cruelly, often the most intellectually gifted – believe there is nothing else. We become hostages of our own stories and forget that we are telling them ourselves. If we are lucky, we sometimes succeed – by trial or chance – to *relax the constraints* of the story, so the absurd may emerge in archetypal forms and speak to us. This is, by any measure, a great and significant achievement. But as liberated from the straitjacket of classical logic, physics, and all that is entailed by our consensus world-instantiation as it may be, *the absurd is still a story*. These meaningful, living metaphors from the unconscious reveal deeper secrets about the nature of our condition as living beings, but they are still self-created myths.

When one finally, and precariously, succeeds in shutting out the story-telling perhaps for a brief moment, one 'jumps out of the system,' as Hofstadter put it.[1] One then has a chance to survey the process of story-telling while standing outside it. The idea is *to go beyond the absurd, and into the Formless*: the part of being that is pure potential, undifferentiated into any myth or storyline. What insights might that perspective entail? What might the Formless have to tell us?

Once one intellectually buys into the worldview we have been articulating, it becomes impossible *not* to attempt a certain exercise: to imagine what the perspective of the Formless might entail. As I have discovered, there is something liberating about it, so I will share my attempt with you for what it is worth. Naturally, in order to *communicate* my imagined message of the Formless through language, I have no alternative but to make a story out of it. This defeats the point somewhat, but hopefully not completely. The story form I chose is that of an imaginary letter sent to me by 'the Formless.' It goes like this...

Rejoice, for I am from a world beyond the farthest reaches of your rational modeling. In my home, a subject is merely a moving viewpoint in a maelstrom of perceptions, feelings, and ideas; like a sliding pair of eyes trained at the *inside* of the body that is Creation. From here, your logic, your science, but also your conceptions of life, death, and soul, are but cartoons: flattened, simple, infantile stories conjured up by a sweet childhood of thought in a desperate search for closure. A gaping abyss stretches out between the images they evoke and the recursive, self-referential landscapes I watch unfold as I drift along the stream of qualia that I am.

Your life is a patchwork of projected concepts; a thin conceptual crust around an unfathomable core of the amorphous substance of existence. Logic – which you create by channeling and constricting the flow of this substance – exists only in the crust. Lifting the rug of logic can take you closer to the *secret* behind what you call reality: the self-referential nature of all conscious experience. He who cracks this secret witnesses in awe the shattering of consensus reality into a million pieces. As these pieces fall to the ground, like a broken mirror, he is confronted with the unspeakable: the most alien and yet most familiar of all realizations.

But this is a realization you have not yet reached, just glimpsed from a ludicrously long distance. So immersed are you still in conceptual patchworks, so submerged in the manifested stream of your being, that you cannot see that which you have always known but forget every time you awake to the sleep of life. Still, this is how it should be. Your condition is the epitome of life, for you are going to die, and I am not. Rejoice, for I am you, yet I transcend you.

It is a saddle of your condition that you think only in terms of references and categories you are comfortable with, even when you intuit the existence of that which transcends these references and categories. Anguished by your mortality, you ponder about the survival of awareness beyond bodily death. You conceptualize a ghost-like 'soul,' existing in time and space, which 'leaves' the locus of the physical body upon death as if it were circumscribed by this physical body. You intuitively recognize the cartoonish naïveté of these models, and try to justify them to yourself by postulating 'subtle energies' and other ill-defined physical metaphors that help you hide your ignorance from yourself. Yes, these metaphors have their place, and some may even be the closest you can come to the truth with your limited language. But they are as literal and space-time-bound as the conceptual constructs they supposedly transcend. The aspects of being that 'survive' death and transcend physical existence are as alien to the references and categories of your waking life as your waking life is alien to the references and categories of your dreams. Your attempts to define the transcendent are as hopeless as a dreaming man's attempt to define his physical body as an entity within his dream. Alas, the body is outside the dream and cannot be thought of in terms of the circumstances of the dream! In the same way, that which is transcendent and eternal in you escape the references and categories of your conceptual reality and cannot be conceived as a construct within it.

Yet your life is itself a dream. The problem is that you got it the wrong way around: the dream is not in the body; it is the body that is in the dream. All metaphors, all cartoons of explanation and closure, exist only in the dream. When you sleep, you partially awake. But 'Who is It who dreams?' I hear you ask. This question is itself a reflection of your myopia; your infantile need to conceive of everything as being produced by something else. You see, *the Dreamer is Itself the dream*. The dream is the eternal unfolding and expression of the Dreamer to Itself. And it encompasses countless, perhaps unending viewpoints within it; viewpoints which the Dreamer assumes, and which entail amnesia from all other perspectives.

Yes, every realm in the unfathomable dream of existence rests on layers upon layers of amnesia. Without identifying with a viewpoint, and forgetting who you really are, you could not taste from the many cups of experience. What finality or limitation could you know were it not for your forgetfulness? What weight could your actions carry? What significance could your achievements or failures hold? Rejoice for your ability to forget, for it endows you with the colors of life. But bear this in mind: you will once again remember. And when you do, you will again be home. In the interim, live out your myths – imaginatively.

Chapter 9

The shape of things to come

Jung observed that all that resides in the unconscious levels of the psyche seeks its way to the surface: to become known in metacognitive awareness. This process is central to psychic health: only through the harmonious integration of unconscious contents into the light of awareness can one achieve individuation and become a complete personality. Moreover, as Jung suggested, there appears to be no other way to harmony and completion but through individuation. As such, it is an inexorable process we all constantly undergo, slowly and imperceptibly as it may be.[1]

Now, insofar as the world is a manifestation of mind and a reflection of the processes it undergoes, we must confront a startling implication: *the universe itself must undergo a kind of 'cosmological individuation' by means of which unconscious world-instantiations progressively emerge into metacognitive awareness, thereby getting absorbed or folded into our consensus world-instantiation.* Here is a way to visualize this: In the context of Figure 2, imagine that the submerged mountain chain is formed by volcanic activity pushing lava up to the top and forming volcanic islands above the surface of the sea. The lava, while stored in the bowels of the Earth, represents formless unconscious contents. When the volcanoes erupt, lava spills onto the surface of the islands, bringing parts of the unconscious worlds into the light of awareness. There they must be integrated, so as to become integral and coherent parts of the landscape. Indeed, Jung himself used this metaphor: 'My deep interior is a volcano, that pushes out the fiery-molten mass of the unformed and the undifferentiated.'[2]

It is natural to think of the scope of this cosmological individuation process as encompassing the whole of humanity. However, since it would be somewhat arbitrary to restrict consciousness to humans alone, its scope might be unfathomably broader. As bridges between conscious and unconscious contents are built in mind, so bridges might appear between what Harpur called daimonic realms and our consensus world-instantiation. Different realms of nature may begin to touch and interpenetrate each other with increasing intensity. Absurdity and ambiguity may increasingly become part of our ordinary waking life. The Trickster may be set loose, as it already seems to be in quantum physics.

Could the more weakly-objective calls of the absurd reflect the sputtering of the story-telling engine of our consensus world-instantiation as unconscious realms begin to subtly erupt from the depths? Could our world be standing on a geological fault line where pressure has been invisibly building up just under our feet? If so, we are inevitably on our way to a future when our most basic assumptions regarding logic and rationality will become untenable; a future that, from our perspective of today, will seem absurd and yet unimaginably meaningful and rich. Here we have reason to hope: we can look forward to the transcendence of our current limitations; to a future when we will look back at the meaninglessness, dryness, purposelessness, and emptiness of our current worldview as illusory, claustrophobic artifacts from a dark age of thought. We may then ask ourselves in bewilderment: How could people live like that back then? What kind of collective delusion was that?

Yet, the path to such a future cannot be a linear and comfortable one. Jung spoke of it once as having the appearance of 'irrational craziness,' an 'absurd disturbance of [his] meaningful human activity.'[3] Indeed, there can be no 'clean' evolution from our current worldview to the scenario sketched above, for a 'clean' evolution entails the progressive gathering of cumulative and unambiguous evidence towards new, rational conclusions. Clearly, this presupposes our present logic and scientific paradigm; it entails bivalence. But it is bivalence itself that will be in dispute. It is the scientific paradigm that, as Kuhn's observations rendered inescapable, will eventually fall. No, we cannot transcend the boundaries of our current rationality through the careful and cumulative taking of rational, clear-cut steps and the solving of problems. *We cannot rationally out-think our rational thinking.* Our advancement will entail not a causally-closed account of nature, but instead a departure from what we consider sound logic. As Harpur remarked, we may have to altogether abandon our current conception of what truth means, if we are to advance.[4]

The next step in our human adventure must be grounded in a new kind of 'illogical' logic: one conducive to ambiguity and according to which constructivism becomes the engine of the world. It will require a difficult – perhaps painful – adaptation of our ego-consciousness and a departure from some of the dearest premises of our scientific worldview. Yet, it does not need to entail a descent into disorder. Rather, it may allow for a broadening of possibilities: the embracing of higher degrees of freedom in the underlying order of reality, which have always been there without acknowledgement. Ours may be a future akin to a dream; a realm where the imagination is less constrained and yet solid, palpable.

The transition to this next major paradigm cannot be something that an authority from the intellectual élite will solemnly pronounce from a podium and reassure us all of. It must, instead, be a process grounded in direct experience. We may each have to be the vent of a volcano from which new degrees of freedom will erupt into awareness. Our responsibility will be that of judicious artists: to mold the hot lava into harmonious, coherent sculptures of thought, while ensuring that we do not find ourselves engulfed and burned in their fiery flow. As Jung said, 'The supreme meaning never dies; it turns into meaning and then into absurdity, and out of the fire and blood of their collision the supreme meaning rises up rejuvenated.'[5]

Chapter 10

What to make of it all?

The calls of the absurd – with their simultaneous contradictoriness, symbolism, and physical reality – have led us to review some of the latest, groundbreaking results coming out of experimental physics. These results, amongst which one finds the experimental confirmation of quantum entanglement and the correlations between global mind states and physical events, have exposed the untenability of realism. As such, the world 'out there' is not independent of the thoughts 'in here.'

In examining the implications of the defeat of realism, we have concluded that we must also abandon the principle of bivalence in logic; that is, the notion that things must be either true or false. Indeed, without realism there is no correspondence theory of truth to ground bivalence. Things can indeed be true *and* false, physical *and* imaginary, so long as we *construct* them to be so. We have thus been led to intuitionistic logic and constructivism as, respectively, a coherent mode of reasoning and a worldview that remain consistent with all the latest experimental results, as well as with the calls of the absurd. We have discovered that reality is the outcome of a coherent mental construction, whose coherence constraints nonetheless do not leave much room for relativism. The historical review of the evolution of scientific thought, as done by Thomas Kuhn, seemed to confirm all this.

Upon the realization that subjective psyche and objective world are likely two aspects of the same thing, we have delved into depth psychology in the hope of finding a less epiphenomenal map of nature than physics. We have found it in the rich work of Carl Jung, who discovered the complexities and unfathomable depth of the unconscious layers of our mind. The implication was clear: next to our ordinary consensus world-instantiation, we must all partake of other world-instantiations, despite not being metacognitively aware of them. These other world-instantiations are intrinsically paradoxical and mythopoetic. The calls of the absurd may be but protrusions of these normally unconscious world-instantiations into the ordinary field of awareness. As such, they are both psychological and physical.

The insights acquired from these apparently incommensurable threads of investigation have come together in a surprisingly consistent manner: the constructivism apparent in the historical observations of Kuhn can be explained by the defeat of realism coming out of physics laboratories; Jung's empirical observations of the contradictoriness of the unconscious are consistent with the lack of bivalence underlying the intuitionistic logic we found at the foundation of reality; the metaphorical language of the unconscious, as expressed in the world's fairy tales, finds uncanny correspondence with the symbolical character of the calls of the absurd. Indeed, the empirical insights of depth psychology regarding the absurd nature of the unconscious seem to independently confirm the conclusions we have derived from physics and analytic philosophy, regarding the nature of reality. The consistency and mutual confirmation across all these independent threads is intriguing.

So we are now left with a worldview where logic is itself a construct of mind, not a strongly-objective truth lying in a platonic realm. Rationality is a thin, limited crust around an unfathomable core of the unformed; the meaningful irrational; *the realm of the imagination*. Yet the word 'irrational' must be read with care: here it does not denote foolishness – that is, the lazy neglect of logic – but the very *transcendence* of the limits of logic. *The irrationality of our worldview exceeds and goes beyond logic.*

We all instinctively look for solid references to ground our thoughts, judgments, and decisions. We need neutral and reliable foundations to build our lives upon. Some of us find these foundations in ethics and morals; others, in science and rationality; yet others, in religion or mythology. Still, we all seem to, implicitly as it may be, rely on logic as the ultimate glue holding these various foundations together. Hence, when acknowledging that logic is itself a construct of our imagination – a self-created set of limits – we may feel as though the rug were pulled from under our feet. What references are we then left with to tell meaning from foolishness? Will we be condemned to live out our lives in disorder and meaninglessness? What grounds can we find to guide our future views and choices?

Answering these questions adequately may be the greatest challenge lying in wait in our future. Indeed, it may be the most formidable challenge humanity has yet confronted. And, like many great challenges, it may also represent the greatest opportunity we have ever had to shape our own existence: an opportunity to remold the very fabric of truth.

Plato identified truth with beauty. For him, the true was indeed the beautiful. So here may lie an important clue: if the desacralization of logic pulls the rug of truth-as-we-have-known-it from under our feet, we still have beauty to guide our way. *Aesthetics transcends logic; it comes from deep within the bowels of the mountain chain.* The foundations of our future may be aesthetical: that which inspires and feeds the soul; that which is conducive to happiness and harmony. The basis of our collective judgment as a culture may need to be transmuted from logic to that which guides the hand of an artist. And this does not need to be so difficult: deep inside, we all have an innate, intuitive notion of what is harmonious, beautiful, and fulfilling; if only we can give this innate impulse unfiltered and unbiased expression.

There is no denying that the path to the transcendence of logic can be an arduous one. Multiple deadly mines may lie buried on its road: relativism, disorder, foolishness, paranoia, and insecurity, to name only a few. Yet, traversing it could also be a fulfilling and fun journey: Have you ever noticed how the amusing element of puns is their ambiguity and double meaning? Puns defy bivalence and literal interpretations, this being the very reason why they are funny. *They show beyond doubt that ambiguity is inherently fun, light-hearted, and pleasing.* The transcendence of bivalence can be a reason for fun and laughter at least as much as it can be a reason for distress. Ultimately, it may all depend on the inner attitudes we bring to the process.

The death of bivalence comes hand in hand with the death of its twin brother, realism. As we traverse the cosmological individuation path towards the absurd – not the meaningless – we will find ourselves in a reality of mind; in the realm of the imagination. Some surprises may lie on our way: Who is to say that the islands of ego-consciousness representing terrestrial life are not just a local archipelago among many others? How can we be sure that, connected to the same submerged mountain chain but located way over the horizon, there are not countless other peaks forming countless other archipelagos? If so, then these other archipelagos may have their own weakly-objective consensus world-instantiations, entirely different from ours. Indeed, this would lend an intriguing new twist to the scientific idea of parallel universes and other dimensions, as well as to the religious idea of inhabited spiritual realms. Moreover, since all these archipelagos are but saliencies of the very same mountain chain of mind, we may all be, deep inside, intrinsically connected to those other consensus world-instantiations; just not 'tuned' into them at a metacognitive level. As we progress towards cosmological individuation, confronting more and more of the contents of our unconscious mind, it may sometimes not be trivial to distinguish between private world-instantiations and occasional access to these other, hypothetical consensus world-instantiations from over the horizon. Will we be able to tell a personal reverie from an accidental tuning into alternative world-instantiations created and inhabited by beings whose existence currently lies beyond our knowledge?

The metaphor of submerged mountain chains and

volcanic islands should not be construed as implying that ego-consciousness is the most advanced configuration of consciousness, everything else being somehow inferior or more primitive. No. Instead, the metaphor should be taken at a global level: the mountain chain occupies the crust of the planet – the surface of a sphere. The islands of ego-consciousness are located at the outer reaches of this sphere, farthest from its center. The center of the sphere is, if you will, the center of the mandala of existence; the very source of the geothermal energy that shapes and changes the entire geology of the organism it metaphorically represents. The deepest reaches of the unconscious are the center of gravity of all existence. The contents of the unconscious are not the most primitive or the most advanced; they are merely closer to the origin of all things; to the core of who we are and of what reality is.

The demise of realism will force some very concrete issues on us. Finding itself in a reality of mind will force our culture to awaken to a level of responsibility we have entirely forgotten: we will no longer be able to look upon ourselves as victims of a dispassionate external world. Countless assumptions we have grown used to will need to be revised. For instance, our culture associates *perception* with objects 'out there,' in the external world, while assuming that *emotions* and *ideas* are generated 'in here,' inside our heads. Without realism, such a dichotomy is fallacious: the subject is merely a moving viewpoint in a stream not only of perceptions, but also of emotions and ideas. Just as we walk through a forest, taking in its sights and sounds, we navigate through a stream of emotions and insights; forests of qualia where every tree is a very human emotion; trees of insight, despair, love, hate, bliss. We may have to get used to the idea that, rather than 'having' thoughts and feelings, we 'navigate through' thoughts and feelings in the exact same way we navigate through perceptions.

Our consensus world-instantiation is a metaphor *of* mind *for* mind; a self-referential 'strange loop.' Like an Escher drawing, it does not have one true explanation and meaning to the exclusion of all others. Instead, it is a collective story designed to evoke a journey through experience, emotion, insight. In a way, it may be like a movie: When we watch a movie where, at the end, multiple explanations for the events of the plot are suggested but none is ever made explicit, we are content with the experience despite not knowing the 'real' explanation. We know full well that there is no such thing in a movie; that it is not just that we did not get to see the elusive explanation, but that it was never written, scripted, or shot in film; that the director himself did not know what it was because it never existed; *it was never the point.* And we are fine with it, because we nonetheless had a meaningful and enjoyable experience watching the movie. *Now that was the point.* A movie is simply the carrier of an experience and the trigger of reflections. When we go to a theater, we know – hopefully – that such an experience is itself the goal, not the triumphant disclosure of an elusive, literal explanation for all events of the plot.

For instance, a movie that has been very significant to me personally is Krzysztof Kieślowski's 1991 masterpiece, *La double vie de Véronique* (The Double Life of Véronique). The story is about two apparently unrelated young women – both played superbly by the unequalled Irène Jacob – one living in Poland, the other in France. They are physically identical, share many personality traits, and seem to intuit each other. Their lives seem somehow linked in an acausal manner. Though they are not aware of each other's existence, they are very important to one another at an unconscious level. This provides the framework for a profound and very human storyline. Yet, at no point in the movie does Kieślowski bother to explain the actual relationship between these women or the metaphysics of their connection. Indeed, for anyone absorbing the movie, these explanations are *utterly irrelevant*: it simply does not matter whether they are twins separated at birth, whether they have extrasensory perception, or any of these banalities. The viewer is captured in a captivating, deeply subjective journey, which literal explanations like these would actually spoil. It is the experience of *that* journey that matters, not literal closure. Could we ever look upon reality with the same maturity with which we watch movies like *La double vie*?

While the triumphant *discovery* of a final, causally-closed explanation may not be the reason for the movie of our consensus world-instantiation, the *chasing* of this explanation may well be the engine of its unfolding; the key driver of its plot. Make no mistake, this is a very special kind of movie: in it, we are not just audience, *we are the characters too*; in it, we give ourselves bodies to ground our localized viewpoint; we even give ourselves brains that match the form of our metaphorical understanding of our own mental processes – *mirrors of our myths about ourselves*. Unlike the people in a movie theater, we watch this movie from *within*. As audience, we do well to know we are dealing with metaphors. But as characters, we do well to chase explanations; otherwise the movie would grind to a halt. What else could we do but live out our myths? Yet, we may be able to *choose* our myths and sculpt the storyline so it fulfills our deepest, truest, most beautiful aspirations.

Like actors who deeply internalize the experiences and emotions of their characters, we play our roles exceptionally well. So well, in fact, that it has become nearly impossible for us to transcend the plot. The movie has become a dream we seem unable to wake up from. But all is not lost: as Gödel did, we can break the spell from within, exposing the untenability of any literal interpretation of the movie. We can be like a dreamer who looks in the mirror, sees a face different from his own, and exclaims in astonishment: 'It is a dream!' *This has been the exploratory attempt of this book.* Yet, while we can expose the myth from within, we cannot access what lies beyond it unless we personally step out of the screen; until we actually wake up from the dream, fleetingly as it may be. Gödel showed that no formal system can consistently derive all truths about numbers, but this gave him no insight into those inaccessible truths. He could demonstrate that there is surely something beyond the horizon, but could not see what it is. Gödel was, after all, a character inside the movie, a dreamer inside the dream.

It is important, though, not to misconstrue the implications of the worldview we have developed here. This worldview does *not* imply that the ego-consciousness we ordinarily experience and identify ourselves with can change reality at will, not even if we could completely control and focus our conscious thoughts. Such misinterpretation is based on the false but common premise that we are our egos. The implication of our articulation is, instead, that the psyche *as a whole*, conscious and unconscious parts, personal and collective parts, is the architect of reality. For as long as we are not aware of, and therefore have no explicit control over, what goes on in the unconscious depths of our mind, our ability to change reality will always be limited. It is the whole mountain chain of mind that creates reality, not the ego-consciousness viewpoints of the islands. The latter are probably more like spectators than creators. Indeed, perhaps this is their very *raison d'être*, the very reason why the islands exist and have come to forget what they are part of. Only through cosmological individuation – whereby the universal mind becomes explicitly cognizant of its true and complete Self – can we truly realize our full potential as creators of the drama of existence.

When we think of the future, we tend to imagine amazing new technologies that will vastly improve our lives and reach into the universe. Some of us even foresee that technology will enable us to live indefinitely and solve practically every problem society currently faces.[1] As someone who has been involved in the development and deployment of new technologies most of his life, I have instinctive sympathy for such views. Yet, in light of our discussion, they seem to overlook the elephant in the room. Without bivalence and realism, technology as we know it is an unnecessarily difficult, limited, and precarious way of going about realizing our aspirations as a society. Through technology we build – with great difficulty – structures out of a limited set of predefined, cumbersome building blocks, while all along being intrinsically able to create whatever customized building blocks we want. But we ignore this latter possibility and take great pride in our strenuous efforts to wrestle with nature. Indeed, technology as we know it represents the leveraging of the laws of logic and physics as they currently exist. Yet the ultimate technology is the leveraging of *mind*: the fountainhead of the world; the origin of all logic and physics. If only we could learn to gain mastery of our own mind, conscious and unconscious, unfathomable new possibilities would open up before us.

Could other civilizations, beyond our knowledge or ability to conceive of, have reached the mastery of the technologies of mind? If so, what could their relationship to us be? More importantly, how could we make steps towards the mastery of such technologies ourselves? Do the calls of the absurd offer us clues? The absurd is, and has always been, an intrinsic part of our world. As a culture, we ignore its significance at our own peril. After all, there may just be profound meaning in absurdity.

Epilogue

As a final thought, the ideas expressed in this book are themselves just stories. And these stories, like the semantic paradoxes we have seen earlier, contradict themselves: they deny the literal truth of all models of reality, including their own; they have been woven – analogously to Gödel's theorem – according to the very logic they show to be fundamentally limited. Therefore, the ideas discussed here cannot be literally true. Rather, they are paradoxical and self-negating like the archetype of the Trickster. But then again, this is the very point of this book! This book is itself an integral part of the elusive 'strange loop' of the world; the Escher drawing of existence. What to make of this conundrum is, ultimately, up to you alone.

Notes

Chapter 1

1 At the time this book was written, the footage could be retrieved from a film archive at http://www.hessdalen.org/.

2 See, for instance: G. S. Paiva and C. A. Taft, 'A Hypothetical Dusty-plasma Mechanism of Hessdalen Lights,' *Journal of Atmospheric and Solar-Terrestrial Physics*, Vol. 72(16), doi:10.1016/j.jastp.2010.07.022, October 2010, pp. 1200–1203; and: B. G. Hauge, 'Optical Spectrum Analysis of the Hessdalen Phenomenon, Preliminary Report,' The 7th European SSE Meeting, Norway, August 17–19, 2007.

3 B. G. Hauge, 'Transient Luminous Phenomena in the Low Atmosphere of Hessdalen Valley, Norway,' The 8th European SSE Meeting, Italy, August 13–16, 2009, p. 65.

4 M. Teodorani, 'A Long-Term Scientific Survey of the Hessdalen Phenomenon,' *Journal of Scientific Exploration*, Vol. 18(2), 2004, p. 246.

5 M. Teodorani, *op. cit.*, 2004, p. 245.

6 M. Teodorani and G. Nobili, 'EMBLA 2002 – An Optical and Ground Survey in Hessdalen,' 2002, retrieved from http://www.hessdalen.org/reports/EMBLA_2002_2.pdf, p. 16.

7 Erling Strand, 'Project Hessdalen 1984 – Final Technical Report,' 1984, retrieved from http://www.hessdalen.org/reports/hpreport84.shtml.

8 See, for instance: Joseph Allen Hynek, Philip J. Imbrogno, and Bob Pratt, *Night Siege: The Hudson Valley UFO Sightings*, Llewellyn Publications, 2nd expanded edition, May 1998.

9 See: Carl Gustav Jung, *Flying Saucers: A Modern Myth of Things Seen in the Skies*, Princeton University Press, 1978, pp. 55–62.

10 Carl Gustav Jung, *op. cit.*, 1978.

11 See, for instance: Roderick Main, 'Religion, Science, and

Synchronicity,' Harvest: *Journal for Jungian Studies*, Vol. 46(2), 2000, pp. 89–107; and: C. A. Meier (editor), *Atom and Archetype: The Pauli / Jung Letters, 1932–1958*, Princeton University Press, 2001.

12 See, for instance: João de Marchi, *The Immaculate Heart: The True Story of Our Lady of Fátima*, Farrar, Straus and Young, 1952.

13 See: Rick Strassman, *DMT: the Spirit Molecule*, Park Street Press, 2001, p. 188.

14 See, for instance: R. Strassman, S. Wojtowicz, L. E. Luna, and E. Frecska, *Inner Paths to Outer Space: Journeys to Alien Worlds through Psychedelics and Other Spiritual Technologies*, Park Street Press, 2008.

15 Rick Strassman, *op. cit.*, 2001, p. 221.

16 Rick Strassman, *op. cit.*, 2001, p. 314.

17 Jacques Vallée, *Passport to Magonia: From Folklore to Flying Saucers*, Neville Spearman, 1970, pp. 23–31.

18 Jacques Vallée, *op. cit.*, 1970.

19 Graham Hancock, *Supernatural: Meetings with the Ancient Teachers of Mankind*, Arrow Books, 2006.

20 John E. Mack, *Passport to the Cosmos*, Three Rivers Press, 1999, pp. 159–160.

21 John E. Mack, *op. cit.*, 1999, pp. 287–290.

22 John E. Mack, *op. cit.*, 1999, p. 26.

23 See: Carl Gustav Jung, *The Red Book* (*Liber Novus*), W. W. Norton & Company, 2009, pp. 237–238.

24 See: Carl Gustav Jung, *Memories, Dreams, Reflections*, Fontana Press, 1995, p. 217.

25 See: Carl Gustav Jung, *op. cit.*, 1995, pp. 207–208.

26 See: Carl Gustav Jung, *op. cit.*, 2009, pp. 238–240.

Chapter 2

1 Jacques Vallée, *The Invisible College: What a Group of Scientists Has Discovered about UFO Influences on the Human Race*, E. P.

Dutton, 1975, pp. 17-18.

2   Jacques Vallée, *op. cit.*, 1975, p. 60.

3   Jacques Vallée, *op. cit.*, 1975, p. 108.

4   Jacques Vallée, *op. cit.*, 1975, p. 124.

5   Jacques Vallée and Eric Davis, 'Incommensurability, Orthodoxy and the Physics of High Strangeness: A 6-layer Model for Anomalous Phenomena,' appearing in: *Actas do Forum Internacional 'Ciência, Religião e Consciência,'* Porto, Portugal, 24 October 2003.

6   See, for instance: Jacques Vallée, *op. cit.*, 1975, p. 140.

7   Jacques Vallée, *op. cit.*, 1975, pp. 196–201.

8   Jacques Vallée, *op. cit.*, 1975, p. 196.

9   Jacques Vallée, *Messengers of Deception: UFO Contacts and Cults*, Daily Grail Publishing, 1979.

10 John E. Mack, *Passport to the Cosmos*, Three Rivers Press, 1999, pp. 287–290.

11 John E. Mack, *op. cit.*, 1999, p. 290.

12 John E. Mack, *op. cit.*, 1999, pp. 55–57.

13 John E. Mack, *op. cit.*, 1999, p. 6.

14 Patrick Harpur, *Daimonic Reality: A Field Guide to the Otherworld*, Pine Winds Press, 1994, p. xvi.

15 Carl Gustav Jung, *Dreams*, Routledge Classics, 2002, p. 41.

16 Carl Gustav Jung, *op. cit.*, 2002, pp. 35–36.

17 Patrick Harpur, *The Philosophers' Secret Fire: A History of the Imagination*, The Squeeze Press, 2009, p. 5.

18 Patrick Harpur, *op. cit.*, 2009, pp. 3–5.

19 Patrick Harpur, *op. cit.*, 1994, p. 193.

20 Patrick Harpur, *op. cit.*, 1994, pp. 133–143.

21 Patrick Harpur, *op. cit.*, 1994, p. 89.

22 Patrick Harpur, *op. cit.*, 2009, p. 44.

23 Patrick Harpur, *op. cit.*, 1994, p. xx.

24 More on this in later chapters.

Chapter 3

1 See, for instance: Samir Okasha, *Philosophy of Science: A Very Short Introduction*, Oxford University Press, 2002, pp. 58–76, for a brief but judicious introduction to the contemporary philosophical debate around realism, idealism, and anti-realism.

2 This was the way Samir Okasha described how an anti-realist might view the world. The statement does not necessarily represent Okasha's own personal views. See: Samir Okasha, *op. cit.*, 2002, p. 65.

3 Larry Laudan has listed dozens of examples in his article 'Demystifying Underdetermination,' in: J. A. Cover and M. Curd (editors), *Philosophy of Science: The Central Issues*, W. W. Norton & Company, 1998, pp. 320–353.

4 Technically, the detectors are polarizers that measure the polarization of the incoming photon along a predefined direction.

5 For instance, each detector can measure the polarization of the respective photon along a different direction.

6 Technically, the property here is the particular direction of polarization of the photon.

7 That is, the particular direction of polarization it assumes.

8 Technically, the direction of polarization taken on by the first photon instantly determines, at a distance, the direction of polarization taken on by the second photon.

9 Technically, the correlation depends on the relative angle between the orientations of the two polarizers.

10 See: A. Einstein, B. Podolsky, and N. Rosen, 'Can Quantum-Mechanical Description of Physical Reality Be Considered Complete?' *Physical Review*, Vol. 47, 1935, pp. 777–780.

11 See: J. S. Bell, 'On the Einstein Podolsky Rosen Paradox,' *Physics*, Vol. 1, 1964, pp. 195–200. A more recent collection of Bell's writings on the topic can be found here: J. S. Bell, *Speakable and Unspeakable in Quantum Mechanics: Collected*

Papers on Quantum Philosophy, Cambridge University Press, 2004.

12 Technically, he worked out, for all relative angles between the orientations of the two polarizers, the statistical implications of any hidden variables theory regarding the correlation of measurements.

13 See the following papers: Alain Aspect *et al.*, 'Experimental Tests of Realistic Local Theories via Bell's Theorem', *Physical Review Letters*, Vol. 47(460), 1981; Alain Aspect *et al.*, 'Experimental Realization of Einstein-Podolsky-Rosen-Bohm Gedankenexperiment: A New Violation of Bell's Inequalities,' *Physical Review Letters* 49(91), 1982; and Alain Aspect *et al.*, 'Experimental Test of Bell's Inequalities Using Time-Varying Analyzers,' *Physical Review Letters*, Vol. 49(1804), 1982.

14 See: W. Tittel, J. Brendel, H. Zbinden, and N. Gisin, 'Violation of Bell Inequalities by Photons More Than 10 km Apart,' *Physical Review Letters*, Vol. 81(17), doi:10.1103/PhysRevLett.81.3563, 1998, pp. 3563–3566.

15 See: G. Weihs, T. Jennewein, C. Simon, H. Weinfurter and A. Zeilinger, 'Violation of Bell's Inequality under Strict Einstein Locality Conditions,' *Physical Review Letters*, Vol. 81(23), doi:10.1103/PhysRevLett.81.5039, 1998, pp. 5039–5043.

16 That is, the orientation of the respective polarizer.

17 See: Alain Aspect, 'Bell's Inequality Test: More Ideal Than Ever,' *Nature*, Vol. 398, 18 March 1999, pp. 189–190.

18 Alain Aspect, *op. cit.*, 1999, p. 190.

19 See: Simon Gröblacher *et al.*, 'An Experimental Test of Non-Local Realism,' *Nature*, Vol. 446, doi:10.1038/nature05677, 19 April 2007, pp. 871–875.

20 At the time this book was written, the GCP had a website at: http://noosphere.princeton.edu/. For a description of the experiment design, see: Peter Bancel and Roger Nelson, 'The GCP Event Experiment: Design, Analytical Methods,

Results,' *Journal of Scientific Exploration*, Vol. 22(3), pp. 309–333, 2008.

21 See, for instance: R. D. Nelson, D. I. Radin, R. Shoup, and P. A. Bancel, 'Correlations of Continuous Random Data with Major World Events,' *Foundations of Physics Letters*, Vol. 15(6), doi:10.1023/A:1023981519179, 2004, pp. 537–550.

22 Roger D. Nelson, 'Is the Global Mind Real?' *EdgeScience*, No. 1, October 2009, p. 8.

23 See, for instance: Gerard 't Hooft, 'Entangled Quantum States in a Local Deterministic Theory,' arXiv:0908.3408v1 [quant-ph], 24 August 2009.

24 See, for instance: John G. Cramer, 'The Transactional Interpretation of Quantum Mechanics,' *Reviews of Modern Physics*, Vol. 58, July 1986, pp. 647–688.

25 See: Lee Smolin, *The Trouble with Physics: The Rise of String Theory, the Fall of a Science, and What Comes Next*, Houghton Mifflin Harcourt, 2006.

Chapter 4

1 Bernardo Kastrup, *Dreamed-up Reality: Diving into Mind to Uncover the Astonishing Hidden Tale of Nature*, O-Books, 2011.

2 Bernardo Kastrup, *Rationalist Spirituality: An Exploration of the Meaning of Life and Existence Informed by Logic and Science*, O-Books, 2011.

3 See, for instance: Hans Albert, *Treatise on Critical Reason*, Princeton University Press, 1985.

4 Graham Priest, *Logic: A Very Short Introduction*, Oxford University Press, 2000, p. 6.

5 Douglas R. Hofstadter, *Gödel, Escher, Bach: An Eternal Golden Braid*, Penguin Books, 1979, p. 192.

6 Roger Penrose *et al.*, *The Large, the Small, and the Human Mind*, Cambridge University Press, 2000, p. 1.

7 Roger Penrose *et al.*, *op. cit.*, 2000, p. 2.

8 Stephen Read, *Thinking about Logic: An Introduction to the*

Philosophy of Logic, Oxford University Press, 1995, p. 11.

9 Douglas R. Hofstadter, *op. cit.*, 1979.

10 See, for instance: Susan Haack, *Philosophy of Logics*, Cambridge University Press, 1978, Chapter 8.

11 Stephen Read, *op. cit.*, 1995, p. 158.

12 Graham Priest, *In Contradiction: A Study of the Transconsistent*, Oxford University Press, 2nd edition, 2006.

13 Here I am talking about human languages in general – their linear, sequential, cross-referential structure that is so conducive to closed-loop paradoxes, as well as their tendency towards categorization. I am not discriminating between particular instances of language, such as English or Chinese.

14 See, for instance: Donald Davidson, 'Thought and Talk,' appearing in: S. Guttenplan (editor), *Mind and Language*, Oxford University Press, 1975, Chapter 1. I provide this reference here merely as a substantiation of the assertion made in the main text that belief systems depend, at least to some extent, on language structures. I do not necessarily subscribe to the entirety of Davidson's argument in this article.

15 For a short but careful and well-articulated overview of self-reference and its implications for logic paradoxes, see: Graham Priest, *op. cit.*, 2000, Chapter 5.

16 Douglas R. Hofstadter, *op. cit.*, 1979, p. 21.

17 Here I use the expression 'language games' to refer to semantically paradoxical statements; thus not in the particular sense that Ludwig Wittgenstein used the same expression in *Philosophical Investigations*.

18 See: Kurt Gödel, *On Formally Undecidable Propositions of Principia Mathematica and Related Systems*, Courier Dover Publications, 1992.

19 See, for instance, Wikipedia's article on Escher's *Metamorphosis II*. At the time this book was written, this

article could be retrieved from: http://en.wikipedia.org/wiki/Metamorphosis_II.

20 Douglas R. Hofstadter, *op. cit.*, 1979, p. 15.

Chapter 5

1 Michael Dummett, 'The Philosophical Basis of Intuitionistic Logic,' appearing in: Michael Dummett, *Truth and Other Enigmas*, Harvard University Press, 1978, p. 228.

2 Zen Buddhists would correctly disagree with this, pointing at their koans as proof. By acknowledging this here, I am contradicting what I wrote in the main text. But then again, the view of reality articulated in this book embraces contradiction, so I am not really contradicting myself after all.

3 See, for instance: Stephen Read, *Thinking about Logic: An Introduction to the Philosophy of Logic*, Oxford University Press, 1995, Chapter 8.

4 As cited earlier: Roger Penrose *et al.*, *The Large, the Small, and the Human Mind*, Cambridge University Press, 2000, p. 1.

5 See: Michael Dummett, 'Realism,' appearing in: Michael Dummett, *Truth and Other Enigmas*, Harvard University Press, 1978, Chapter 10.

6 See, for instance: Carl Gustav Jung (author) and Joan Chodorow (editor), *Jung on Active Imagination*, Princeton University Press, 1997.

7 Andries P. Engelbrecht, *Computational Intelligence: An Introduction*, John Wiley & Sons, 2nd edition, 2007, p. 359.

8 See, for instance, Chapter 17, 'Ant Algorithms,' of: Andries P. Engelbrecht, *op. cit.*, 2007.

9 See, for instance: Philip Clayton and Paul Davies (editors), *The Re-Emergence of Emergence: The Emergentist Hypothesis from Science to Religion*, Oxford University Press, 2006.

10 Here I mean chaos in the sense of manifestations free from the constraints of physics and even logic. One can talk of

chaos in the sense that the world often appears disorderly and highly entropic, but then one is still talking about manifestations within the constraints of logic and the laws of physics.

11 This wonderful little derivation can be found here: Ian Stewart, *Professor Stewart's Cabinet of Mathematical Curiosities*, Profile Books, 2008, pp. 37–38.

12 Patrick Harpur, *Daimonic Reality: A Field Guide to the Otherworld*, Pine Winds Press, 1994, p. 174.

13 See, for instance: D. P. Walker, *Spiritual and Demonic Magic: From Ficino to Campanella*, Pennsylvania State University Press, 2000.

14 Thomas S. Kuhn, *The Structure of Scientific Revolutions*, University of Chicago Press, third edition, 1996.

15 William James, *The Principles of Psychology*, Henry Holt and Company, 1890, p. 488.

16 See: Thomas S. Kuhn, *op. cit.*, 1996, p. 17.

17 See, for instance: Graham Priest, *Logic: A Very Short Introduction*, Oxford University Press, 2000, Chapter 11.

18 Thomas S. Kuhn, *op. cit.*, 1996, p. 2.

19 Thomas S. Kuhn, *op. cit.*, 1996, p. 113.

20 See: Samir Okasha, *Philosophy of Science: A Very Short Introduction*, Oxford University Press, 2002, p. 88.

21 Thomas S. Kuhn, *op. cit.*, 1996, p. 94.

22 Thomas S. Kuhn, *op. cit.*, 1996, p. 111.

23 See: Thomas S. Kuhn, *op. cit.*, 1996, p. 193.

24 See: Thomas S. Kuhn, *op. cit.*, 1996, p. 115.

25 See, for instance: Larisa V. Shavinina (editor), *The International Handbook on Innovation*, Elsevier, 2003, p. 440.

26 See: Thomas S. Kuhn, *op. cit.*, 1996, p. 117.

27 See: Immanuel Kant, *Critique of Pure Reason*, Cambridge University Press, 1999.

28 Thomas S. Kuhn, *op. cit.*, 1996, p. 77.

Chapter 6

1 Carl Gustav Jung, *Four Archetypes: Mother, Rebirth, Spirit, Trickster*, Routledge, 2003, pp. 12–13.

2 Carl Gustav Jung, *op. cit.*, 2003, pp. 14–18.

3 Carl Gustav Jung, *op. cit.*, 2003, pp. 159–179.

4 Carl Gustav Jung, *Psychology and Alchemy*, 2nd edition, Routledge, 1968, p. 16.

5 Carl Gustav Jung, *op. cit.*, 1968, p. 25.

6 Carl Gustav Jung, *op. cit.*, 1968, p. 11.

7 Carl Gustav Jung, *op. cit.*, 1968, pp. 157, 190.

8 See: Carl Gustav Jung, *Memories, Dreams, Reflections*, Fontana Press, 1995, p. 208.

9 Carl Gustav Jung, *The Red Book (Liber Novus)*, W. W. Norton & Company, 2009, p. 250.

10 Carl Gustav Jung, *op. cit.*, 1968, p. 50.

11 Carl Gustav Jung, *op. cit.*, 1968, p. 41.

12 Carl Gustav Jung, *op. cit.*, 1968, p. 19.

13 Carl Gustav Jung, *op. cit.*, 1968, p. 182.

14 Carl Gustav Jung, *Dreams*, Routledge Classics, 2002, p. 80.

15 See: Marie-Louise von Franz, *Archetypal Patterns in Fairy Tales*, Inner City Books, 1997; as well as: Marie-Louise von Franz, *The Interpretation of Fairy Tales*, revised edition, Shambhala, 1996.

16 Marie-Louise von Franz, *op. cit.*, 1996, pp. 27–28.

17 Marie-Louise von Franz, *op. cit.*, 1996, p. 45.

18 See, for instance: Marie-Louise von Franz, *Individuation in Fairy Tales*, Shambhala, 1990.

Chapter 7

1 Carl Gustav Jung, *Mysterium Coniunctionis*, Princeton University Press, 2nd edition, 1977.

2 Patrick Harpur, *The Philosophers' Secret Fire: A History of the Imagination*, The Squeeze Press, 2009, p. 32.

3 Readers of my earlier book, *Dreamed-up Reality*, should notice

that these archetypal story patterns correspond roughly to the 'elemental thought patterns' I discussed in that work.

Chapter 8

1   Douglas R. Hofstadter, *Gödel, Escher, Bach: An Eternal Golden Braid*, Penguin Books, 1979, pp. 37–38.

Chapter 9

1   It is possible, and even likely, that in the historical past this process was in fact reversed: that humans have experienced a separation between previously integrated aspects of their psyche, leading to the formation of the unconscious. This is an exceedingly interesting topic that, nonetheless, is outside the scope of this book. Here, we will consider only what appears to be the current course of the process: from a highly disintegrated psyche to a progressively more integrated one, through the inexorable process of individuation.

2   Carl Gustav Jung, *The Red Book (Liber Novus)*, W. W. Norton & Company, 2009, p. 247.

3   Carl Gustav Jung, *op. cit.*, 2009, p. 291.

4   Patrick Harpur, *Daimonic Reality: A Field Guide to the Otherworld*, Pine Winds Press, 1994, p. xxi.

5   Carl Gustav Jung, *op. cit.*, 2009, p. 230.

Chapter 10

1   See, for instance: Ray Kurzweil, *The Singularity Is Near: When Humans Transcend Biology*, Viking Adult, 2005.

BOOKS

ACADEMIC AND SPECIALIST

Iff Books publishes non-fiction. It aims to work with authors
and titles that augment our understanding of the human
condition, society and civilisation, and the world or universe in
which we live.
If you have enjoyed this book, why not tell other readers by
posting a review on your preferred book site.

Recent bestsellers from Iff Books are:

Why Materialism Is Baloney
How True Skeptics Know There is no Death and Fathom Answers
to Life, the Universe, and Everything
Bernardo Kastrup
A hard-nosed, logical, and skeptic non-materialist metaphysics,
according to which the body is in mind, not mind in the body.
Paperback: 978-1-78279-362-5 ebook: 978-1-78279-361-8

The Fall
Steve Taylor
The Fall discusses human achievement versus the issues of war,
patriarchy and social inequality.
Paperback: 978-1-90504-720-8 ebook: 978-184694-633-2

Brief Peeks Beyond
Critical Essays on Metaphysics, Neuroscience, Free Will,
Skepticism and Culture
Bernardo Kastrup
An incisive, original, compelling alternative to current mainstream
cultural views and assumptions.
Paperback: 978-1-78535-018-4 ebook: 978-1-78535-019-1

Framespotting
Changing How You Look at Things Changes How
You See Them
Laurence & Alison Matthews
A punchy, upbeat guide to framespotting. Spot deceptions and
hidden assumptions; swap growth for growing up. See and be free.
Paperback: 978-1-78279-689-3 ebook: 978-1-78279-822-4

Is There an Afterlife?
David Fontana
Is there an Afterlife? If so what is it like? How do Western ideas of the afterlife compare with Eastern? David Fontana presents the historical and contemporary evidence for survival of physical death.
Paperback: 978-1-90381-690-5

Nothing Matters
A Book About Nothing
Ronald Green
Thinking about Nothing opens the world to everything by illuminating new angles to old problems and stimulating new ways of thinking.
Paperback: 978-1-84694-707-0 ebook: 978-1-78099-016-3

Readers of ebooks can buy or view any of these bestsellers by clicking on the live link in the title. Most titles are published in paperback and as an ebook. Paperbacks are available in traditional bookshops. Both print and ebook formats are available online.
Find more titles and sign up to our readers' newsletter at
http://www.johnhuntpublishing.com/non-fiction
Follow us on Facebook at
https://www.facebook.com/JHPNonFiction
and Twitter at https://twitter.com/JHPNonFiction